WRITE IN THE MIDDLE

Andrea C. Downing

A Guide to Writing for the ESL Student

WRITE IN THE MIDDLE

A Guide to Writing for the ESL Student

Connie Shoemaker

SPRING INTERNATIONAL LANGUAGE CENTER
ARAPAHOE COMMUNITY COLLEGE

Holt, Rinehart and Winston, Inc.
Fort Worth Chicago San Francisco Philadelphia
Montreal Toronto London Sydney Tokyo

Publisher   Charlyce Jones Owen
Acquisitions Editor   Vince Duggan
Senior Project Manager   Sondra Greenfield
Senior Production Manager   Nancy Myers
Art Director   Judy Allan
Text Designer   Rita Naughton
Cover Designer   Joan Peckolick

Library of Congress Cataloging-in-Publication Data
Shoemaker, Connie.
    Write in the middle: a guide to writing for the ESL student
Connie Shoemaker.
    p.   cm.
    1. English language—Rhetoric.   2. English language—Textbooks for
foreign students.   I. Title.
PE 1408.S4876 1989
428.2'4—dc19

ISBN 0-03-006508-9

Printed in the United States of America
  0   1   2 090 9   8   7   6   5   4   3

Holt, Rinehart and Winston, Inc.
The Dryden Press
Saunders College Publishing

Copyright acknowledgments are on page 241.

DEDICATION

To those students who have developed the understanding that they and their international classmates are all part of the same family—the human family.

Preface

Writing the preface to a book is somewhat like launching a newly built ship with the crack of a champagne bottle. A first voyage . . . adventure . . . effervescence.

Write in the Middle is launched with the goal of guiding the intermediate ESL student through the sometimes troubled waters of writing in a second language. With this aim in mind, the text sails under the colors of the process approach to writing, a method that leads students to experience the adventure of discovering ideas and recording them in writing. The underlying premise of the book is that writing is a process that can be learned by practicing the actions of the good writer. It is assumed that the instructor's responsibility is to help student writers develop a process that will not only allow them to write to express their individual ideas but also to develop their patterns of thinking and learning. That is to say, the instructor is a guide, a fellow writer, an editor, and an expert resource person.

Who Is the Book For?

The book is designed to bridge the gap between the guided writing necessary for beginning ESL students and the independent writing assigned to college and university students. In other words, it is for those students who are "right in the middle" of their English language study. In fact, the writing of this book received its impetus from the needs of teachers expressed in writing workshops facilitated by the author over the past 10 years. "How can I assist my students to move from controlled writing to the kinds of writing required in the college classroom?" was a question often asked by the ESL instructors in these workshops.

Write in the Middle is suited to students in an intensive English program or in an ESL program at a college or university. It has been classroom tested in both situations.

How Does the Book Achieve Its Purpose?

Write in the Middle is able to accomplish its goal by blending a strong process approach with the best of previous product-oriented techniques acquired by the author during 25 years of teaching writing in this country and abroad.

Each of the first nine chapters uses photographs and quotations from world writers to stimulate students' ideas about a central topic. Through the use of journal writing, brainstorming, freewriting, and other techniques of invention, students are encouraged to put these ideas on paper. Students become an active community of writers, discussing, reading, writing, and responding to each other's ideas—in English, the target language. They are then guided through the other actions in the process: focusing, supporting their thesis, and, finally, revising and refining what they have written. Grammar, punctuation, and sentence-combining exercises grow out of the needs of each type of composition focused on in the chapters.

Student compositions, many of which demonstrate the various stages of the writing process, give examples that are achievable and interesting to students of varied cultural backgrounds. Each chapter ends with revision exercises, suggestions for journal writing topics, and additional composition ideas. A supplementary chapter features a thorough treatment of paraphrasing and summarizing, skills absolutely essential to college-bound students.

The *Instructor's Manual* that accompanies the book offers assistance by providing suggestions and guidelines for each of the individual and group exercises in the book, in addition to suggestions on organizing course work for 9-week, 12-week, and semester-length terms. Guidelines are provided for responding to student writing, for grading of writing assignments, and for selecting and organizing groups for collaborative learning.

ACKNOWLEDGMENTS

I would like to express my gratitude, first of all, to Dr. Mark Clarke who encouraged me several years ago to put my ideas about teaching writing into textbook form. My deepest appreciation goes to the entire staff at Spring International Language Center, Arapahoe Community College, for its encouragement and support, and its willingness to accept my manuscript for classroom testing. Finally, I am grateful to the following colleagues for their helpful reviews of the manuscript: Jo-Len Braswell, Wayne State University; J. D. Brown, University of Hawaii; Irwin Feigenbaum, University of Texas at Austin; Virginia D. Lezhnev, Georgetown University; Carol Pineiro, Boston University; Barbara Lindsey Sosna, University of Arizona; Kenton Sutherland, San Mateo Community College; Elizabeth Templin, University of Arizona; Kathy Trump, Northern Virginia Community College, Annandale Campus; Marcellette G. Williams, Michigan State University; and Jean Zukowski/Faust, University of Arizona.

My husband, Floyd, and children, Sonja, Melissa, and Troy, also deserve my heartfelt thanks for their interest in my project and for allowing me to drop out of family activities when deadlines approached.

CONNIE SHOEMAKER

Contents

WRITE IN THE MIDDLE

A Guide to Writing for the ESL Student

CHAPTER 1

A Process of Discovery

At last . . . made wonderful discovery in valley. . . .

—Howard Carter, discoverer of King Tut's tomb

INTRODUCTION TO THE PROCESS OF WRITING

In 1922, Howard Carter discovered the place where King Tutankhamun was buried in the Valley of the Kings in Egypt. Many steps had to be followed before this important discovery was made. First of all, Lord Carnarvon, a rich Englishman, got the idea that there might be an unknown burial place in the valley. He made a plan after studying maps of the other places where Egyptian kings were buried. Then he hired a young man, Howard Carter, to help him dig in the places that looked most promising. They worked for more than five years before Carter found the 16 steps that led down into the famous tomb of King Tut.

Writing Is a Process of Discovery

As a writer, you can make important discoveries, too. Your discoveries will not be made by digging into the rock and sand, as Howard Carter did. Instead they will be made by "digging into" your thoughts. If you are able to sort through your ideas about a topic and find connections between them, you may discover an idea which is new to you, one that you have never thought of before.

Writing Is a Process You Can Learn

Writing what you want to say in a new language is not always easy. First you learn to hear a new language, to read it, and to understand its grammar. Then comes writing, which is a skill you must work to develop. You can learn to write well in English if you start now to practice the steps in the process of writing. Soon you will be able to explain your thoughts clearly and to share your discoveries with your readers.

STEPS IN THE PROCESS OF WRITING

Getting Ideas   Focusing on a Main Idea   Supporting that Idea   Writing the First Draft

Revising   Drafting Again

When you follow the steps in the writing process, you do not have to follow the order shown in the illustration on page 3. For example, you may get ideas, choose one and try to support it with facts, only to find that you do not have enough support. Then you have to go back and choose another idea to focus on, revise the wording of that idea, and then look for support.

To improve your understanding of writing as a process, let's look at the five steps an intermediate ESL student followed in writing a short composition. The instructor had assigned a composition of between two and three paragraphs on what each student missed the most about his or her country.

Getting Ideas

Before he started to write, Jae Whon, who is from Korea, made this list of all the things he missed about his country and family. He used a spiral notebook to record his ideas. This notebook became his journal.

What I Miss Most

family	playing cards with friends
Korean food—kimchee	big city—lots to do
my girlfriend	my car
my mother's cooking	father—smell of cigarettes
my 3-year-old sister	my own bed upstairs
being taken care of by my	having dinner ready for me
mom and big sister	when I came home
my father's good advice	clean clothes everyday

Focusing

When he read over the list of ideas, he considered for a moment and added another, more general idea that included some of his other thoughts: "the love and care of my family." Next he crossed out the things on his list that didn't fit this major idea: "the love and care of my family."

This is what his list looked like after he had focused on one idea and crossed out the things that didn't support that idea:

What I Miss Most

family
Korean food—kimchee
~~my girlfriend~~
my mother's cooking
my 3-year-old sister
being taken care of by my
    mom and big sister
my father's good advice
~~playing cards with friends~~

~~big city—lots to do~~
~~my car~~
father—smell of cigarettes
my own bed upstairs
having dinner ready for me
    when I come home
clean clothes everyday
(the love and care of
    my family)

Supporting and Drafting

The next thing Jae Whon did was to put his main idea into a full sentence, a thesis for his composition:

Although I been in U.S. for six months I still miss love and care of my family in Korea.

Then he read the sentence aloud. He noticed a mistake in grammar, so he changed the verb tense:

Although I have been in U.S. for six months I still miss love and care of my family in Korea.

Then Jae Whon looked back at his list of ideas and started to write some other sentences that would support his thesis.

Although I have been in the U.S. for six months, I still miss love and care of my family in Korea. I didn't 깨닫다 how much my family important until I live by myself here in America. I have four people in my family. I have little sister who is old three years. I have big sister also. She is old 22 years. And I have mother and father. When I go to bed at night I have picture in mind. The picture I have in my mind is my father smoking best cigarette he always smoke and sitting in best chair by kitchen table. My mother is cooking rice and chiken on stove. Big sister is taking dishes from shelves on the wall. When I am coming in door my little sister run to me and take me by knees and say "hello."

Revising and Editing

At the end of this paragraph, Jae Whon decided to read it aloud to hear how it sounded. When he did this, he realized that he had forgotten some of the articles—*a*'s and *the*'s—and some of the verbs didn't seem to agree with other verbs he had used. He made these changes and then looked up the Korean word in his dictionary to find out what it means in English. After making these corrections, he added a final sentence to his first paragraph and read it aloud again to find out if it sounded better.

Drafting Again

Jae Whon followed the same process for his final two paragraphs, asked for advice from his teacher on how he might improve the composition, and then wrote his final draft. Here is his completed composition:

Jae Whon Lee
Intermediate Writing
Professor Mendez
March 8, 1988

My Family in Korea

Although I have been in the U.S. for six months, I still miss the love and care of my family at home in Korea. I did not realize how much my family meant to me until I had to live by myself here in America. My family includes four people: two sisters, one who is three years old and one who is twenty-two, and my middle-aged mother and father.

When I go to bed at night, 6,000 miles away from my home, I have a picture of my family in my mind. My father is smoking his favorite cigarettes while he sits in a big wooden chair by the kitchen table. My mother, who has a blue scarf on her hair, is cooking rice and hot spicy chicken on the small stove. My big sister is taking dishes from the shelves on the wall. When I come in the door from school, my little sister runs to me and grabs me by the knees to say "hello." This mental picture sometimes makes me cry, but it also makes me feel the love of my family across the miles.

I really did not appreciate the small things that my family used to do for me when I was living at home. My mother and sister always had a hot meal ready for me when I returned from studying. Now, living by myself here in the United States, I must cook my own meals and that is very difficult since I don't know how to cook well and quickly. In addition, my clothes were always clean and neatly folded instead of piled in the corner waiting to be washed. What I miss the most is having someone to talk to when I need advice. My father was always ready to listen to me and to suggest what I should do. These things my family did for me may seem very small, but all of them expressed love and care, which I now miss very much.

QUESTIONS FOR CLASS DISCUSSION

1. Can you describe the steps through which Jae Whon went to write this composition?
2. Did his steps follow the same order as the diagram on page 3?
3. Did he repeat any of the steps in the writing process? Which ones?
4. What is Jae Whon's thesis sentence?
5. Can you recall three or four details that support this thesis?
6. How does Jae Whon conclude his composition?
7. Is his concluding statement similar to his thesis sentence?

THE FORM OF A GOOD COMPOSITION

Writing a composition is like building a house. A builder must have good quality materials to construct a house that will satisfy its owners. The builder also needs a pleasing, neat plan for the house. When you have followed the steps in the writing process, you will have good quality materials, or content, for your composition. In order to finish the composition, so it is interesting and pleasing to the reader, you must write it in a form that is neat and easy to understand. The form of a composition is important because it shows the reader what you want him or her to know.

Here is an acceptable form for a short composition.

Your name—Juanita Flores
Class name—Intermediate Writing
Date —— September 18, 1987

Title correctly
capitalized—A Good Composition

Paragraph indented

A good composition is interesting, well-organized, and clearly — thesis
written. First, a composition cannot be interesting unless it has good
ideas. Ideas are the life-blood of any kind of writing.

A composition must also be well-organized. In American-style
writing, a focus or thesis should be clearly stated early in the
composition. Then the focus should be supported with examples, facts,
descriptions, or anecdotes. The supporting sentences make the reader — Support
believe the truth of the focus statement. Finally, the composition must
have a conclusion.

Clearness in writing is the third characteristic of a good
composition. Clearness comes from choosing correct words; using proper
grammar, spelling, and punctuation; and showing the relationship of
ideas. To be considered excellent, a good composition must have these — Conclusion
three characteristics: interest, organization, and clarity.

USING THE WRITING PROCESS

You have studied a student example of the steps in the writing process. Now it is time for you to try the process yourself.

EXERCISE 1-1   What Do You Like Best About Studying in the United States?

Follow the steps in the writing process to compose one good paragraph about this topic.

1. **List**   Making a list of your ideas is one of the ways to begin the writing process. In our everyday lives we use lists to remind us of things we have to do. Many times when a writer makes a list, one idea leads to another idea. Listing also helps the writer to see his ideas. He can then circle or underline important ideas, or number or draw connecting lines between ideas.

What I Like about Studying in the United States

_____

_____

_____

_____

_____

_____

2. **Focus**   Read over your list of ideas. Is there an idea in the list that seems to be a focus for the other ideas? If so, circle this idea. Do some of the ideas seem to be related or to fit together? How are these ideas related? Connect the related ideas with lines. Write in a few words that show how they are related. Now, what is the major idea about studying in the United States that best explains your other ideas? Write this main idea here:

_____

_____

_____

3. **Support**   What ideas on your list will support your main idea? Are there other facts or examples that would add support to your main idea? Add these to the list. Now rewrite the ideas on your list in the order that you want to talk about them.

1. _____

2. _____

3. _____

4. _____

5. _____

6. _____

4. **Draft**   State your main idea in a complete sentence. Begin your paragraph with this sentence. Use the numbered ideas to form other sentences that will support your main idea. Use a separate piece of paper for your draft.

5. **Revise**   Read aloud what you have written. Are your sentences clear? Do they all seem to fit together smoothly? Do you have enough sentences to support your main idea? After making additions or corrections, have a class-mate read your paragraph and comment on it. Can he or she suggest other changes?

6. **Draft Again**   Write your paragraph a final time. Choose a title. Indent the first sentence and write on every other line of the notebook paper. Check your work against the example of a good composition on page 8. Give your second draft to the instructor for comments. After you have looked over your instructor's comments, enter the major mistakes in the chart, "My Editing Checklist," on page 243.

Hints for Drafting

1. Find a quiet place to write—use a clean desk or table.

2. Have sharpened pencils, pens, and lots of paper ready.

3. Plan your writing at a time when you will not be interrupted by phone calls, visits from friends, or favorite TV programs.

4. Place your "idea sheets" (lists, brainstorming, and so on) near you, so you can easily refer to them.

5. As you write, leave extra lines and wide margins, so that you have room to make corrections and additions.

6. Try to write down everything you want to include in your composition in one sitting. Do not worry about order of ideas, grammar, spelling, or punctuation. Just work at getting everything possible down on paper. You can make revisions later.

7. If you plan to give your draft to the instructor, be sure it is easily readable. If it is not, recopy it.

EXERCISES TO POLISH UP YOUR WRITING

7. **Proofread**   The final step in writing your composition is to proofread it. Proofreading is like cleaning your apartment or house, so it is neat and looks well-cared for. When you proofread, you clean up mistakes in grammar, punctuation, and spelling.

   In the paragraph, "What I Like about Studying in the United States," your instructor may have noticed some mistakes in word order, verb tenses, complete sentences, or punctuation. The exercises that follow will help you to improve, or "polish up," your composition.

EXERCISE 1-2   Choosing Correct Verb Forms

In the paragraph you have just finished writing, you gave some opinions about studying in the United States. If you are saying how you feel about studying now, you will need to use the **present tense** or one of its forms.

EXAMPLE

> The thing I most **like** about the United States **is** its freedom. I **have** the freedom to live where I **choose,** to study in any university that **accepts** me, and to choose the major I **like** best.

However, if you give examples in your paragraph of events that happened in the past, you will need to change your verbs to **simple past tense** or one of its other forms.

EXAMPLE

> When I **was studying** in my country, I **had** to choose the major that **fit** the score on my final high-school exam.

Fill in the blanks in the following paragraph with the correct form of the verb in parentheses.

Colorado: My Favorite State

Colorado _____ (to be) my favorite state because of its climate and

its weather. The state _____ (to have) very little rain, which _____ (to

give) it a dry, sunny climate. In fact, there _____ (to be) more than 325

days of sunshine every year. This kind of climate _____ (to seem) very

different from my country, Thailand. For example, last year in Thailand we

_____ (to have) 32 days in a row without sunshine. This kind of dreary

weather _____ (to make) me wish to travel to a place where I _____

(to be able to) see the sun.

Now that I _____ (to live) in Colorado, I _____ (to know) what it is

like to have a winter season. In the winter here, it _____ (to snow), but

there _____ (to be) sunshine when it isn't snowing. Colorado _____

(to give) me this variety. Some people _____ (to say), "If you don't like

the weather in Colorado today, it _____ (to change) by tomorrow." In my

opinion, it is the changes in weather that _____ (to make) this state

interesting.

EXERCISE 1-3 **More Practice with Verb Forms**

In some of the exercises in this book, you will be asked to write about your country, your culture, or your family. If you are writing about these topics as they are **now,** you will want to use **simple present tense.**

EXAMPLE

My family **includes** three brothers and one sister.

If you, like Jae Whon in the composition at the beginning of this chapter, are describing actions that are taking place in your thoughts, use the **present continuous.**

EXAMPLE

I have a picture of my family in my mind. My father **is sitting** at the kitchen
table.

My Favorite Beach

The beach closest to my home in Caracas, Venezuela _____ (to

be) Mirabelle. This white, sandy beach _____ (to look and to smell)

clean and beautiful. There _____ (to be) cool breezes which

_____ (to blow) across the sand and _____ (to make) a rustling

sound in the tall palm trees. When I _____ (to be) at home in Vene-

zuela, I _____ (to go) to Mirabelle Beach for every school holiday.

When I am in a difficult situation here in the United States, I can see that

beach in my mind. The breeze _____ (to blow) across my face, the

waves _____ (to roll) onto the beach, and the sun _____ (to

warm) my shoulders.

COMPLETE SENTENCES

When you write your ideas in a composition, you want them to be understood
clearly by the reader. Your ideas will be clear if you express them in complete
sentences.

**A complete sentence is a group of words that has at least one
subject and one verb and that makes sense by itself.**

Complete sentences can be short.

EXAMPLE

He sat down.

Complete sentences also can be made much longer by adding more than
one subject or verb and by adding phrases (word groups without subjects and
verbs).

EXAMPLE

Every evening he wrote a letter to his parents, called his girlfriend, and then
just sat in front of the TV set.

Learning to recognize complete sentences will help you to write your own
thoughts clearly.

EXERCISE 1-4 Recognizing Complete Sentences

Some of the groups of words in this exercise are complete sentences and some
are not. Write **C** on the blank line beside each group of words that you think is a
complete sentence. In each group of words marked **C,** underline the <u>subject</u>

once and the <u>verb</u> twice. Place end punctuation (. ? !) at the end of complete sentences.

EXAMPLE
  American <u>homes</u> <u>have</u> several TV sets

___ 1. Television is an important part of American life

___ 2. At least two television sets and sometimes more

___ 3. Adults watch TV an average of two hours per day

___ 4. Children under 5 years old watch from three to four hours per day

___ 5. If children watch educational programs

___ 6. Their vocabulary and knowledge of the world

___ 7. Do American children watch the best programs

___ 8. TV is a babysitter

___ 9. A variety of activities for the young child

___ 10. Watching television is only one of the important activities for a growing
      child

THE DANGER OF SENTENCE FRAGMENTS

As you check the answers to the previous exercise, you will notice that four of the word groups were not complete.

> **Groups of words that do not express a complete thought are called fragments.**

It is easy to forget to finish a sentence. Writers sometimes make the mistake of writing part of a sentence, a fragment, as though it were a whole sentence, able to stand by itself with a capital letter at the beginning and a period at the end. The fragment usually happens when the writer stops too soon and leaves the end of the sentence standing by itself.

EXAMPLE

> Fragment: Their vocabulary and knowledge of the world will grow. **If children watch educational programs.**

The second group of words in the previous example is not a new thought; it is a way of developing the idea in the basic sentence before it. It tells **how** their vocabulary and knowledge will grow.

> Corrected: Their vocabulary and knowledge of the world will grow if children watch educational programs.

A fragment like the one in the example is very common because it has its own subject and verb that looks like a sentence (children watch); however, this group of words actually tells why, how, when, or where the action in the previous sentence took place. It does not tell that something actually happened. Such groups of words are clauses. They usually begin with words such as *because, since, when, if, as,* or *while*. These are **danger words** that tell the writer to beware of a fragment. When you begin sentences with these words, be certain that they refer **ahead** to the main part of a new sentence, **not back** to the sentence before. Notice this difference:

EXAMPLE

> Fragment, Danger word referring backward: TV is a babysitter. **Because it gets children's attention and keeps them quiet.**

> Complete sentence, fragment attached: TV is a babysitter **because** it gets children's attention and keeps them quiet.

> Two Complete sentences, danger word referring ahead: TV is a babysitter. **Because** it gets children's attention and keeps them quiet, parents often tell them to sit and watch a program.

The last three sentences in the example above are complete sentences. In the sentence with the fragment attached, *because* tells why TV is a babysitter. In the last sentence, *because* tells why parents tell children to watch TV programs. In both sentences *because* explains something in the same sentence.

Danger words are connectors; they can refer both ways. If you begin a sentence with one of them, make the word refer ahead; otherwise, keep it in the same sentence.

EXERCISE 1-5   Changing Fragments to Complete Sentences

On the blank line beside each group of words, write **C** if it is a complete sentence, or **F** if it is a fragment. Rewrite each fragment to make it a complete sentence by adding words that complete the thought. Add end punctuation.

EXAMPLE

F 1. Although pets are not common in some countries

___ 1. More than half of American homes have pets

___ 2. If an American has a dog

___ 3. Pets usually are not kept outdoors

___ 4. Because I am afraid of large dogs

___ 5. Since I live by myself

___ 6. I like small, clean animals

___ 7. The biggest household pet I have ever heard of

___ 8. When I was a child

___ 9. Birds, like parakeets and finches, are my favorite pets

___ 10. Since I have come to the United States, I have grown to like both dogs and cats

___ 11. I will have a small dog if I ever have a pet

___ 12. Not many people in my country have dogs because they are not considered clean

EXERCISE 1-6 Punctuating Complete Sentences

End punctuation helps the reader to know when a thought is complete. Put **periods** or **question marks** in the correct places in the following paragraph to mark the end of complete ideas. Add **capital letters** to mark the beginning of each new sentence.

Quiz Shows

American TV has many different types of programs I like the quiz show best the quiz show is like a contest average people can try to answer questions they win prizes and try their luck on the jackpot the jackpot is a big sum of money or other kinds of prizes that go to the top winner maybe someday I will be the jackpot winner on an American quiz show what do you think

A CLOSER LOOK AT IDEAS AND FOCUS

Ideas in a composition are like oxygen to the lungs. The composition cannot exist without ideas, just as the human being cannot live without oxygen.

Brainstorming

There are many ways to start ideas flowing. What follows is a group of ideas that are organized in a diagram with the topic in the center and related ideas arranged around it. As you can see, other ideas have grown out of the major ideas. This diagram is the result of **brainstorming**. Brainstorming simply means letting one idea lead to another. It is usually a group activity in which one person writes down the ideas as members of the group quickly offer them.

Study the ideas that a group of Lebanese students generated.

QUESTIONS FOR CLASS DISCUSSION

1. What are the students' five major ideas?

2. Why did they connect other lines to these ideas?

3. Why do you think they drew a line from "freedom to choose major and college" to "things are bad at home"?

1. A BRAINSTORMING DIAGRAM

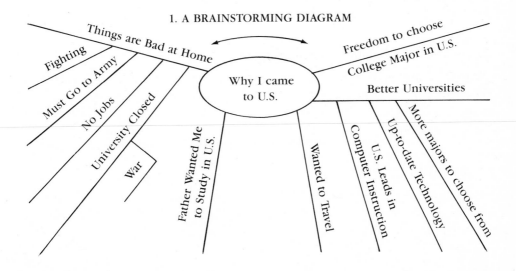

4. Which of the students' ideas seems to be the strongest or easiest to write about?

5. Are any of the ideas related? Could they be combined into one idea?

Freewriting

A good way to get many ideas in a short time is to **freewrite.** A good place to do this freewriting is in an 8½ x 11 spiral notebook that you use for freewriting only. This notebook will become your journal. Simply start writing and keep on writing for 5 to 10 minutes without stopping. Don't go back and look at what you've written and don't worry about correct spelling, grammar, or punctuation. Just keep on writing ideas as fast as you can. If you can't think of anything, write, "I can't think of anything to say" until some more ideas come. This method of getting ideas will help you to discover hidden ideas that you didn't know about before. Freewriting also helps you develop fluency in English, in other words, the ability to use the language easily.

Focusing

Focusing means centering on one idea and then expressing an attitude or opinion about it. If you were writing a paragraph from the ideas above, what would you focus on? How does your focus relate to the topic "Why I Chose to Come to the United States"? State that relationship in one complete sentence.

Focusing is one of the most difficult but most important elements in good writing. Every paragraph must have a main idea, and every composition needs a thesis statement. Both the main idea and the thesis statement are ways of focusing on a topic. A clear statement of focus is part of the American style of writing.

> **The focus of a paragraph is called a main idea.**
> **The focus of a composition is called a thesis statement.**

EXERCISE 1-7   **Practice Focusing Ideas**

Write focus statements from the following groups of ideas using the techniques mentioned.

1. A list of ideas

Differences Between Food in My Country
and the United States

France	*United States*
more flavor and spices	not many spices
sauces	food is too plain
food takes long time to prepare, so it is better	food is cooked too quickly
	no good smells

French are famous for cooking many kinds of pastries more variety of main dishes	not much variety—it all tastes the same

Focus statement: _____

_____

2. A brainstorming diagram

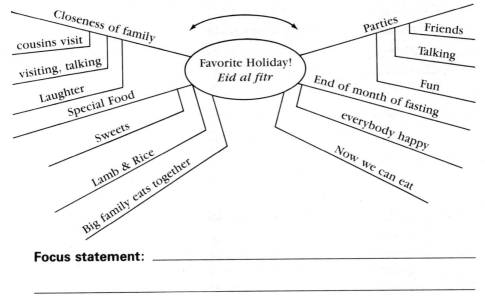

2. A BRAINSTORMING DIAGRAM

MY FAVORITE HOLIDAY

Focus statement: _____

_____

3. A freewriting exercise

Students and professional writers sometimes use freewriting as a way of "freeing up" the flow of ideas. To freewrite students must write as quickly as they can without stopping to think about organization or whether or not the ideas are good. Here's a sample of freewriting from an intermediate student.

I don't like the buses in this town. Buses are a problem here not like in my country. It's so easy to take a bus in my country. It's easy not hard. Why? I don't know. I have to think about that for a minute. Why is it easy at home but hard here? I guess here they don't run very often so I have to stand and wait 30 minutes, sometimes 1 hour. One day I got sick just waiting for the stupid bus. Buses here don't go all the places I want to go and they cost too much money. I can't think of anything else to say?????????????? I don't like the buses, right? Maybe the problem is that the government doesn't run the bus system. I guess it's just run by people or a company a private company. They must not make enough money to run them the right way.

Focus statement: _____

_____

Exercise 1-8   **Writing a Paragraph with Focus and Support**

Choose one of the focus statements from Exercise 1-7 and use this statement as the first sentence of a paragraph. Support this main idea with three to five additional sentences that express ideas from the groups of ideas. Write your main idea and supporting sentences in paragraph form. Read your draft aloud. Revise. Write it again with any changes or corrections.

GROUP EXERCISE

Using a Diagram to Link Ideas

Form a group with three or four students in your class to work on the topic "Culture Shock." Culture shock describes the feelings and problems a person has when he enters a culture or country different from his own.

Each group should choose one person to write down the group's ideas on a large piece of paper. Write this topic in the center of the paper.

Now think of as many ideas as you can that have something to do with Culture Shock. The recorder should write all ideas without stopping to discuss them. If any ideas fit together, try to place them near each other or to draw lines connecting them.

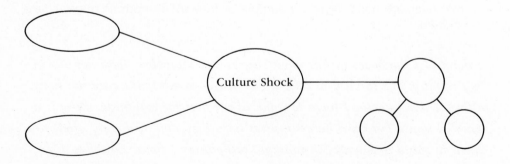

After each group has spent 5–10 minutes recording their ideas, they should discuss their diagram to see if ideas are related. Is there one major idea under which others fit? Use the paper to draw lines between ideas or to circle major ideas.

Now, as a group, try to write a sentence that expresses the main idea or focus of your diagram. Share your diagram and focus sentence with the class.

Exericse 1-9   Writing a Paragraph from the Idea Diagram

Using the ideas and focus statement of your group, write a paragraph of six to eight sentences. Begin with the focus sentence and support it with ideas from the diagram in Exercise 1-8. Follow the remaining steps in the writing process: drafting, revising, and writing for the final time in correct paragraph form.

REVISION EXERCISES

REVISION EXERCISE 1   Adding Focus to a Paragraph

Add focus to the following short composition by writing a sentence that generalizes about the specific ideas in the composition.

My Most Embarrassing Moment

_____

_____

In the bathroom of my American family's home was a pretty, flowered plastic bottle with a plunger on top. Each day, after washing my hands, I would push the plunger and rub some of the creamy liquid over my hands to keep them from getting dry. After five or six days, I noticed that my hands were red and dry. The skin was cracking and even starting to bleed. I asked my family if they could help me to see a doctor about my hands.

"Do you use hand lotion on them?" my American mother asked.

"Yes," I said, "everyday I use lotion from the bottle in the bathroom."

"Oh, dear," the mother replied, "that's not hand lotion. That's liquid soap."

REVISION EXERCISE 2   Deleting Ideas That Do Not Fit

This paragraph includes three ideas that do not support the main idea. (The main idea is in italics.) Cross out the ideas that do not fit.

Discovery Is Hard Work

If Howard Carter and Lord Carnarvon had given up easily, the world would never *have known about the beautiful objects that belonged to King Tutankhamun.* Egyptian officials had told the two British archaeologists that there were no more unknown tombs in the Valley of the Kings. However, this didn't stop Carter and Carnarvon. They decided to search every inch of the Valley. Lord Carnarvon was in Egypt trying to get well after a serious illness.

They started digging before World War I but found that serious work could not begin until 1917. That year they found nothing. They tried searching again in 1918, 1919, 1920, and 1921, but found no tombs. Robbers had taken gold and jewelry from many of the tombs. In the summer of 1922, Carnarvon thought of ending their work. Carter begged him to try one more time. Many other archaeologists had visited and left the Valley of the Kings in the past 20 years. In November of 1922, Carter and his workmen found a step, the first of 16 leading down into the hillside. At the bottom was a doorway. Right away Carter sent a telegraph to Lord Carnarvon: "At last . . . made wonderful discovery in Valley. . . ."

FOR WRITERS WHO HAVE MORE TO SAY

JOURNAL ASSIGNMENT

Write in your journal about an important discovery you have made about yourself or an important discovery you have made about American culture.

CLASS ASSIGNMENT

Use the process of writing to compose a paragraph about one of the following topics:

What I Have Discovered About U.S. Culture

An Embarrassing Moment

Learning a Second Language Is Important

The Most Important Value in My Culture

What Traveling Has Taught Me

CHAPTER SUMMARY

Writing is a process that includes the following steps:

getting ideas

focusing on choosing a main idea

supporting that idea

making a conclusion

writing the first draft

revising

drafting again

proofreading

These steps do not always happen in the same order and some steps may be repeated.

In this chapter, you tried several ways of generating ideas and focusing on main ideas:

listing

brainstorming/diagramming

freewriting

As you continue to write, experiment with using these and other methods of discovering ideas.

The form of a composition, including neat margins, heading, indenting, title, is important because it shows the reader you are serious about your writing and helps him read your work more easily.

CHAPTER 2

A Time to Dance

"A time to weep, and a time to laugh, a time to mourn, and a time to dance."

—Ecclesiastes

Dancing, which is as old as history itself, is part of every culture. It was created by and for the people of each nation. It is also a way of expressing joy, of celebrating, and of telling a story.

JOURNAL ASSIGNMENT

Study the photographs of dancers from different cultures on the preceding pages. Now read the quotation from Ecclesiastes, which is a book in the Bible ("to weep" means to cry; "to mourn" means to feel sad, especially about someone who has died). Think about what this quotation means.

Now that you have spent a few minutes thinking about the theme of this chapter, "A Time to Dance," it is time to write down some of your ideas. Use any or all of the techniques discussed in Chapter 1.

USING THE WRITING PROCESS TO BUILD STRONG PARAGRAPHS

Getting Ideas

Look back over what you have written in your journal notebook. On a new page, write down the best ideas and any new ones that come into your mind as a result of reading your freewriting or thinking about your lists or diagrams. Share the ideas you like best with your class. In fact, your instructor may record all ideas on the blackboard in a diagram like this one:

Focusing
Questions for Class Discussion

1. How many groups of ideas are there in the diagram?

2. Are any of the groups of ideas related to each other? Which ones? Draw lines between them to show that they are related.

3. Is there a general word or words that describes each group of ideas? For example, the general class of ideas already printed on the diagram is called "Definition of Dance." Add these general words to the groups of ideas if they are not already there.

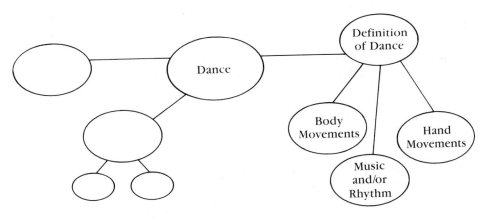

In putting your ideas into this diagram, you have grouped **specific ideas** into more **general classes.**The **specific ideas** are details, such as facts, examples, or personal experiences. The **general classes** are the major groups into which specific ideas fit. When you follow this process of grouping specific ideas into general groups, you are focusing on the controlling ideas for a writing assignment.

Narrowing the Focus

The next step in writing about the topic of dance is to choose one of the groups of ideas as the topic of a paragraph. Now what? You have a good group of ideas that relate to dance. How do you get them into a well-written paragraph? The best way is to follow this formula for a good paragraph:

$$\textbf{main idea + support + conclusion = a good paragraph}$$

What is the general class of ideas you have chosen? (Is it the uses of dance? The differences between dance in various cultures? A definition of dance? Or something else?) This general class is your topic. To write a good main idea you simply need to say something about the topic. Here you would write a sentence that expresses an attitude, an opinion, or a fact about your topic.

EXAMPLE:

> Dancing is an exciting and important part of most social occasions in my country.

Your statement of the main idea can be used as the first sentence of your paragraph about dance, or you may use another sentence that introduces the topic you have chosen and then use the main idea as the second sentence.

EXAMPLE:

The Purposes of Dance

Dance is part of the tradition of every culture in the world. These dances are used by the people of each culture for many different reasons.

Support

Look back at the diagram of ideas on dancing. What can you use from this diagram to support your main idea? Can you add additional ideas to support your main idea? Write a first draft of your paragraph. Conclude the paragraph with a summary or final statement about your topic.

Revise

Read the paragraph aloud to yourself or have a classmate read it. Is it easy to understand? Does it have all the qualities of a good paragraph?

Edit

Look for mistakes in grammar, punctuation, and spelling. Use the Editing Checklist at the end of the book for the mistakes you made in your previous composition. Try not to repeat these mistakes. Make corrections and write the paragraph **again** in the correct form described on pages 7–8.

If you need help understanding what to do when you revise and edit your paragraph, study the following example by Elena from Czechoslovakia.

DRAFTS OF A STUDENT'S PARAGRAPH

First Draft

Dance

I want write about the sentence "A time to weep, and a time to laugh, a time to mourn and a time to dance". This sentence doesn't means dance. I think it talks about life. Life is hard. And life is also times to be sad. Like when someone dies. Life has time to be happy too. Dancing is happy someone dances when they are feeling joy. So this sentence say that life has many parts. Happy parts and sad parts. For example my own life is very happy now. Because helthy and I study to make a new future in the United States. But two year past my life was very sad. Because the goverment take my husband job and I have no work too. It is like someone dead. I was mourn the good times in life.

Second Draft

Elena asked her husband, who was also a student in the class, to read her paragraph. He asked her, "What is your main idea?" Elena said, "My main idea is that the sentence about a time to dance is true about my life, about our lives." Her husband suggested that she put that main idea into her composition as the first or second sentence and also that she end her composition by saying in some other words the same main idea. "Why do you call your paragraph 'Dance'? It really isn't about dance, is it?" Elena's husband asked. Elena agreed. She read her paragraph again and made the following changes:

The happiness and sadness of life

"A time to weep, and a time to laugh, a time to mourn and a time to dance." This sentence from Ecclesiastes means a lot to me because it tells a truth about my life. Sometime life is very hard and we weep. But an other time life is easy and we are happy and laugh. Also there are times we loose people we love or things we like then we mourn and are sad. In the other hand those sad times balanced from times we are so happy we feel like dance. My life is an example of these different parts. I am very happy now. Because helthy and I study to make a new future in the United States. But two year past my life was very sad. Because the goverment took my husband job and I have no work too. It was like someone dead. I was mourn the good times in life. Because I experience all these parts of life I believe that the writer of quotation was very wise.

Third Draft

Next Elena asked her instructor to check the paragraph for mistakes in grammar, punctuation, and spelling. After her instructor had pointed out some mistakes for correction, Elena edited the paragraph and rewrote it for the final time. As she rewrote, she changed a few of the words to say more clearly what she meant.

Elena Zupček
Intermediate Writing
Professor McCarthy
October 27, 1988

The Happiness and Sadness of Life

"A time to weep, and a time to laugh, a time to mourn and a time to dance." This quotation from Ecclesiastes is still as true today as it was thousands of years ago. Sometimes life is very hard and we weep. Other times life is easy, and we are happy and laugh. Also there are times when we lose people we love or things we value. Then we mourn and are sad. On the other hand, those sad times are balanced by times when we are so filled with joy that we feel like dancing. My *life is an example of these different times. I am very happy now because I am healthy and I am studying to make a new future in the United States, but two years ago my life was very sad. The government had taken away my husband's job and I had no work either. I mourned the loss of these important activities as if I was mourning the death of someone close to me. Because I have experienced all of these happy and sad times in life, I believe that the writer of this quotation was very wise.*

You have seen how one student used the writing process to create a paragraph that was easy to understand and enjoyable to read. The following list, "Qualities of a Good Paragraph," will remind you of what you need to include in your paragraphs.

Qualities of a Good Paragraph

1. **A main idea** that states an attitude, opinion, or fact about the topic

2. **Specific support** for the main idea in the form of

   facts—figures, statistics, proven statements;

   examples—single items drawn from a larger group (specific cases of a general idea);

   description—details (size, shape, color,) or a combination of these kinds of support.

3. **A concluding statement** or, if the paragraph is part of a whole composition, a sentence that leads the reader into the next paragraph

4. **Coherence** All sentences fit together smoothly and logically.

EXERCISES TO POLISH UP YOUR PARAGRAPH WRITING

Recognizing the parts of a good paragraph will help you to write well-developed paragraphs of your own.

EXERCISE 2-1   **Recognizing Parts of a Good Paragraph**

In the paragraphs that follow, underline the main idea, put a bracket next to the supporting details, and tell what kind of support is used: facts, examples, description, or a combination of these. Circle the conclusion.

EXAMPLE

One of my most difficult adjustments to American life was getting used to new kinds of food. Since I love rice and hot, spicy foods, it was very hard to enjoy eating bland potatoes and plain beefsteaks and hamburgers. Breakfast was another problem. I had always thought dry cereal and milk was for babies. Where was the rice and fresh papayas or mangoes that I had always eaten for breakfast? After several months of starving myself, I discovered that I could learn to cook my favorite foods. Now I eat a nice combination of American and Thai foods.

Examples

1. The English language is still strong and growing, according to Stuart Berg Flexner, linguist and social historian. English, which has a history of changing rules and growing vocabulary, will continue to change in the next century. The most interesting changes will be in vocabulary. Hundreds of thousands of new words will be added to the more than 750,000 that we use today, while very few words will be dropped. Old English had 50,000 to 60,000 words, and we still use about 70% of them. By Shakespeare's day, another 80,000 to 90,000 words were included in the language, and we continue to use 75% of these.

2. Many people think of Africa as a continent of jungles and lions. This image of Africa, however, is simply not true. Only about 5% of Africa is true jungle. Also most Africans have seen lions only in zoos or game parks. Each area of this huge continent has unique geography, people, problems, and promises. North Africa, for example, includes the Sahara, the world's biggest desert. Most of the 100 million people in this region are Moslems. In Sub-Saharan Africa, there are hundreds of individual religions, languages, and ethnic differences. These are just two examples of areas of Africa that do not fit the usual movie image of this continent.

3. Americans are marrying later today than they did 20 years ago. Statistics show that women in 1966 married at about 20 years of age, and men in that year were about 23 when they got married. Today's statistics show that, on an average, women are marrying at age 23 and men at age 26. This is an increase of three years in age for both sexes.

4. Television has greatly influenced social life in my country. Fifteen years ago, before everyone had television sets and video players, friends and relatives would spend their evenings playing backgammon or cards and visiting with each other about events of the day. Today we sit glued to the television set to watch programs or American video cassettes. We seldom have a long conversation and no longer play the games we used to enjoy. Those good old days of fun and friendly talk will never return.

5. My mother is one of the most caring people I know. "I have never met a person I couldn't like in some way," she frequently says. When she meets people for the first time, she immediately makes them feel comfortable, so that they tell her the most important events in their lives and also share their problems. She truly listens to people. If they tell her that they have a problem, she will help them to solve it. She does not give them solutions but encourages them to find the best way. Because she forgets her own worries and concentrates on the other person, she is truly a caring, loving woman.

TWO PARTS OF A MAIN IDEA

As you discovered in Exercise 2-1, main ideas are central to good paragraphs. What makes a good main idea? A good main idea or topic sentence, as it is sometimes called, has two parts: the **topic** and the **controlling idea.**

> **The topic is what the writer is talking about.**
> **The controlling idea is the word or words in the sentence that**

state an idea or attitude about the topic.
The controlling idea or attitude can also be called a generalization or focus.

EXAMPLE

Mr. Walker is the best teacher I have ever had.
Topic: Mr. Walker
Controlling idea: best teacher I have ever had

Venezuela is a country of great natural beauty.
Topic: Venezuela
Controlling idea: great natural beauty

Now let's practice recognizing the two parts of a main idea or topic sentence.

EXERCISE 2-2   Identifying Parts of a Main Idea

In each of the following main ideas, circle the topic and underline the controlling
idea.

1. (Modern farm equipment) has changed the life of my village.

2. Americans are informal people.

3. Khalil Gibran is my favorite poet.

4. Scientists have found that animals have complicated forms of communication.

5. Calcium is important in the diet of women over 30.

6. Smoking must be prohibited in all public places.

7. This city's pollution comes from heavy downtown traffic.

8. My religion gives me my most important values.

9. A good sense of humor helps me to face life's difficulties.

10. My most important goal is a good education in computer science.

THE CONTROLLING IDEA AND SUPPORT

The controlling idea in a topic sentence or main idea tells the writer what kind of
support is needed to write the paragraph.

EXAMPLE

The Porsche is one of the best-designed cars in the world.

In order to support the controlling idea—best-designed cars—the writer would have to describe its design and the advantages that comes from such a design.

Another main idea might require facts for support.

EXAMPLE

My city is one of the most heavily populated in Asia.

The writer would have to tell how many people live in his city.

EXAMPLE

I believe that education is the key to development of my country.

The writer would have to use examples of how education could develop a country.

EXERCISE 2-3 Supporting Controlling Ideas

For each of the following main ideas, circle the controlling idea and then write out two sentences (examples, facts, description) that support that idea. The first one is done.

1. My uncle is the (funniest person I know)

   a. *He can imitate the voice and walk of*

   many movie stars and other famous people.

   b. *He always makes jokes about himself.*

2. American supermarkets include more than just food items.

   a.

   b.

3. It is very difficult to get a driver's license in the United States.

   a.

b. _____

_____

4. _____ is the most beautiful place I have visited.

a. _____

b. _____

5. My country is located in an important political area of the world.

a. _____

b. _____

6. I firmly believe in the old saying, "Haste makes waste."

a. _____

b. _____

CHECKING FOR UNRELATED IDEAS

In the last exercise, you supported main ideas with sentences that were closely related. When you apply this exercise to your own writing, you will discover that it is helpful to read aloud what you have written to check for unrelated ideas.

In a good paragraph, all details suport the main idea. Sentences that do not fit the main idea are called *irrelevant* sentences. *Irrelevant* means *not related.*

EXERCISE 2-4 Finding Irrelevant Ideas

Find and underline the irrelevant sentences in the following five paragraphs.

1. In American culture, the rose is a symbol of beauty and love. A young man gives roses to his sweetheart to show her how much he loves her. Large bouquets of roses are given to beauty queens, such as Miss America and Miss Universe. The gift of even a single rose shows the person receiving it that someone cares. Roses can be found in many colors and varieties.

2. I admire the Indian leader, Mahatma Gandhi for his strong religious beliefs. Gandhi studied law in Great Britain and then went to South Africa. As a child, Gandhi's mother showed him by her example the value of prayer and religious fasting. In Gandhi's middle years, his reli-

gious beliefs caused him to reject all the pleasures of life for the joys of religion.

3. Tennis is one of the cheapest recreational sports. The only equipment required is a racket and a can of tennis balls. In addition, there are many free tennis courts at parks and schools. It is a sport that provides great aerobic exercise. Very inexpensive lessons can be obtained through local schools and colleges. Since so many people play tennis, it is easy to get a friend to give you a lesson.

4. Many Americans think that the time they spend at work is more important than their leisure time. In a study conducted by the Roper organization, 46% of the 2,000 adults interviewed said that work was more important. The people interviewed lived in all parts of the United States. Thirty-three percent said that leisure time was more important than work, and 17% thought that both work and leisure were equally important. Four percent of those interviewed did not know which area of life was most important.

5. My friend, Somchai, is one of the smartest people I know. When he was in high school, he got a straight *A* average in all subjects. His high-school grades allowed him to enter one of the best universities in Thailand, from which he graduated in just three years. Somchai also plays the guitar and enjoys all kinds of sports. Before coming to the United States, he scored 550 on the TOEFL, which is a test of English proficiency.

These exercises should have helped you to develop a "critical eye," something every good writer needs. Since "practice makes perfect" (an old American saying) let's continue to practice the process of writing good paragraphs.

EXERCISE 2-5   Writing Main Ideas from Details

State the main idea from each group of facts, examples, or descriptive details.

1. In the United States schooling is required until age 16. About two-thirds of the people graduate from high school. Ninety-seven percent finish at least eighth grade. Only one out of every 100 citizens in the United States cannot read or write.

MAIN IDEA: _____

_____

2.

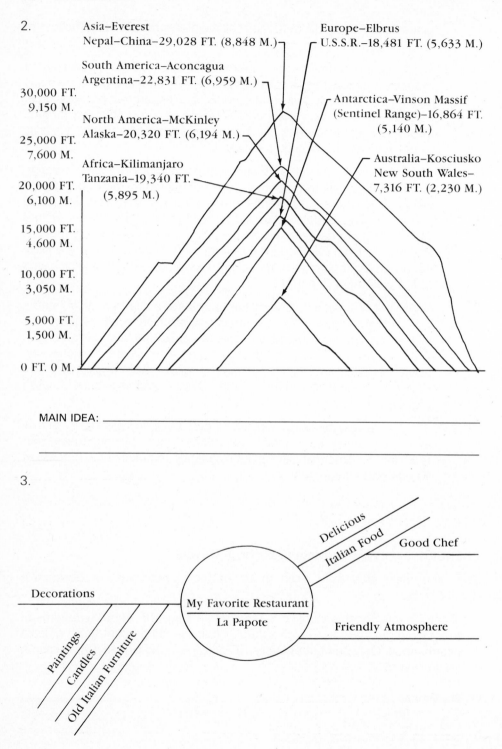

Asia–Everest
Nepal–China–29,028 FT. (8,848 M.)

Europe–Elbrus
U.S.S.R.–18,481 FT. (5,633 M.)

South America–Aconcagua
Argentina–22,831 FT. (6,959 M.)

30,000 FT.
9,150 M.

Antarctica–Vinson Massif
(Sentinel Range)–16,864 FT.
(5,140 M.)

North America–McKinley
25,000 FT. Alaska–20,320 FT. (6,194 M.)
7,600 M.

Australia–Kosciusko
New South Wales–
7,316 FT. (2,230 M.)

Africa–Kilimanjaro
20,000 FT. Tanzania–19,340 FT.
6,100 M. (5,895 M.)

15,000 FT.
4,600 M.

10,000 FT.
3,050 M.

5,000 FT.
1,500 M.

0 FT. 0 M.

MAIN IDEA: _____

_____

3.

Delicious
Italian Food
Good Chef

Decorations

My Favorite Restaurant
La Papote

Friendly Atmosphere

Paintings
Candles
Old Italian Furniture

MAIN IDEA: _____

_____

4.   Margarita

   from Colombia   sang and played on television in Colombia
   plays guitar   favorite pastime is listening to American jazz
   likes to write songs   likes to eat Italian food
   has six sisters

MAIN IDEA: _____

_____

5.   Telephones

  20 years ago—black with white dial
  today—beige, white, green, blue, red telephones
     telephones shaped like Mickey Mouse, Snoopy
     some telephones have calculators, computers,
       built-in address books, and drawers for jewelry

MAIN IDEA: _____

_____

LINKING WORDS

Linking words or expressions link what has come before with what is to follow. Careful use of linking words makes writing coherent.

**Linking Words Used for
Supporting Details in a Paragraph**

  for example   to illustrate (an object must follow this phrase,
  for instance   such as *To illustrate this point*...)
  for one thing   to prove
  let me illustrate   (object must follow)
  as an example   in particular
              specifically
              in addition

Linking words often are used at the beginning of sentences. When used this way, they should be followed by a comma.

EXAMPLE

In addition, Margarita takes modern dance classes.

EXERCISE 2-6   Writing Paragraphs with Linking Words

Using the main ideas and support in Exercise 2-5, write paragraphs for any three of the five groups of ideas in that exercise. In each of your three paragraphs, begin with the main idea and support it with clear sentences. Keep the thought of the paragraph flowing smoothly from sentence to sentence by the use of linking words or expressions.

EXERCISE 2-7   Recognizing Linking Words

Circle the linking words and phrases in the paragraph that follows. Not all of the linking words are used to introduce examples.

Informal Americans

Informality can be seen in many American gestures and much of their other nonverbal communication. For example, placing hands on hips or in pockets while talking is very common. It is also usual to motion with the index finger or with the hands when trying to emphasize an idea. To illustrate further, when Americans are in informal situations, they basically sit as they please—slouched, legs together or crossed, or even with their feet up on a table or desk. In addition, Americans move frequently while they are talking. As you can see, the typical American informality comes out in all aspects of communication.

EXERCISE 2-8   Using Linking Words for Main Ideas

Linking words and expressions, including certain adverbs also are used to introduce main ideas or generalizations

Linking Words Used to Introduce Main Ideas

in general	always
generally	usually
generally speaking	frequently
on the whole	often
in most cases	sometimes
all, every	never
as a rule	seldom

Each of the main ideas below contains a linking word, expression, or adverb that signals a generalization. Complete the sentence.

1. Generally speaking, international students like _____

   _____.

2. As a rule, the TOEFL _____

   _____.

3. Teachers are _____ people. My teacher, for instance,

   always _____.

4. In most cases, universities in my country _____

   _____.

5. Every child must learn _____.

   For instance, when I was a child, I _____

   _____.

6. When I am watching TV, I frequently _____

   _____.

7. It is never a good idea for a traveler to _____

   _____.

8. On the whole, _____ is a good city to live in. For example,

   you can find _____ there.

9. A visitor in my country should never _____

   _____.

10. In general, people in my country _____

    _____ when they meet someone for the first time.

EXERCISE 2-9 Using Linking Words in a Paragraph

Study the list of ideas below. The list was gathered from an interview with a student. Write a paragraph with a main idea, supporting details, and a conclusion. Use linking words to connect ideas.

Salim

From the United Arab Emirates

23 years old

Three sisters, four brothers, his mother and father died when he was 8 years old

Wants to be doctor—studying medicine at University of Southern California

Had polio when he was 12 years old—right leg paralyzed

Worked hard on physical exercises, so now he can walk with just a slight limp

"Even though the pain was great, I did four hours of special exercises everyday until I could walk again."

Made excellent grades in high-school science classes

Worked in hospital with polio patients when he was in high school

Studied two years of premedicine classes in England

REVISION EXERCISES

REVISION EXERCISE 1   Ujung Pandang City

Read the following paragraph, and make the changes suggested at the end.

Ujung Pandang City

Ujung Pandang is the fourth biggest city in Indonesia. Since Indonesia became independent, many people from all corners of the world have come to visit this country. Ujung Pandang is one of several Indonesian cities located on South Celebes Island, which has many beautiful places because of its seas, mountains, and colorful beaches. A favorite place of mine is Losari beach, which is near Ujung Pandang City. This tourist attraction is cool in the hottest weather because of the nearby mountains.

1. Begin the paragraph with a main idea. (The topic is Ujung Pandang City.)

2. Add a controlling idea that expresses an attitude or opinion about the city.

3. One sentence in the paragraph is irrelevant. Take out this sentence.

4. Organize the other information about this city in order of importance.

5. Finish the paragraph with a sentence that states your opinion, in different words than the main idea, of Ujung Pandang City.

6. Use linking words and phrases to connect supporting ideas.

REVISION EXERCISE 2   Time

Read the following paragraph and make the suggested revisions.

Time

One of the student's biggest challenges is using time well. I have some advice about that. Take control of your time by planning ahead. Write important dates on a wall or desk calendar. As soon as an important assignment is made, write it down on the calendar. Put down dates of tests, when papers are due, when midterm exams are scheduled, and so on. Keep a list of things you must do in a notebook that you keep with you at all times. Put your most important daily tasks first. Then as you accomplish a task, cross it out. Set aside definite times to study everyday. Studying is difficult when a student is hungry. Make sure the times you choose to study are when you are alert and rested. Choose a quiet, comfortable study place. It is not advisable to study in the crowded cafeteria or in front of the TV with your friends.

1. This paragraph begins with a good introductory sentence. Rewrite the second sentence, "I have some advice about that", to a main idea that uses *advice about managing time* as the topic.

2. Add a controlling idea that says something about the benefits of taking advice.

3. The writer of this paragraph has four pieces of advice he gives to the student. Let the reader know each time a new piece of advice is being discussed. You can do this through linking words such as *first, second, then,* and so on.

4. One sentence in the paragraph seems irrelevant. Take out this sentence.

5. Finish the paragraph with a sentence that states the advantages of managing time well.

6. Write a more specific title for the paragraph.

FOR WRITERS WHO HAVE MORE TO SAY

Journal Assignment

Do you like to dance or play a specific sport or do some other kind of activity? Why do you enjoy this special activity? How does it make you feel?

Class Assignment

Write a paragraph about one of these topics:

An important person in the history of your country

The value of space exploration

The difficulty of getting a U.S. driver's license

The benefits of having many brothers and sisters

Respect for older people

CHAPTER SUMMARY

A good paragraph includes a main idea that states an opinion, attitude, or fact.

The main idea is supported with specific examples, facts, or description.

A good paragraph has a concluding statement or a sentence that leads the reader to the next paragraph.

The main idea, which is the key to a good paragraph, includes a topic and a controlling idea.

Good paragraphs must be coherent. The main idea and supporting sentences should fit together smoothly and logically. Linking words help to make writing coherent.

CHAPTER **3**
Telling Tales

We'll live, and pray, and sing, tell old tales and laugh.
—William Shakespeare

Storytelling began long before writing was developed. A family or tribe of people would sit around a fire in the evening to tell stories of the hunt or of an important fight that they had won. Later on, when human beings learned to read and write, these stories were recorded in books.

JOURNAL ASSIGNMENT

Was storytelling an important part of your childhood? Do you have memories of someone telling you stories? Write in your journal about these memories.

USING THE WRITING PROCESS

The story continues to be an important part of writing because it lets the reader experience events that he or she may never have the chance actually to live. In addition, it gives the reader a chance to step into someone else's shoes and to feel and act as that person does. Today, writers compose many kinds of stories, or **narratives,** as they are called: the novel, the short story, and anecdotes, which are small stories used to support ideas in many forms of writing.

As a writer of English as a second language, you will need to know how to use the narrative, or story, form in your writing. The major purposes of many kinds of writing are to inform and to explain. Both purposes can be accomplished by telling a brief story. In other kinds of writing, such as description and argument, your main ideas can be nicely supported with narration, or storytelling. In summary, learning to tell stories is useful in all kinds of writing.

QUESTIONS FOR CLASS DISCUSSION

As you look at the photos of storytelling at the beginning of this chapter, you will notice that the people listening to the stories are involved and interested in what the storyteller is saying.

1. What are the qualities of a story that make it interesting to the listener?

2. If you were telling a story to a 5-year-old child, how would you capture his attention? How would you keep him interested in hearing all of the story? What kind of words would you use?

3. If you were telling a story to someone your own age, would you do the same things that you would do with the 5-year-old? If not, what would you do that is different?

4. When you write a story, you cannot change the loudness or softness of your voice as the oral storyteller can. You cannot stop and wait a minute for excitement about the ending to build up in the listeners' minds. What can the writer of stories do to make them interesting to his readers?

THE IMPORTANCE OF YOUR AUDIENCE AND YOUR PURPOSE

Oral storytellers can see their audience, the people listening to them. They can tell right away if someone doesn't understand what they are saying or if the listeners are bored. Good storytellers will watch the faces of their listeners and change the way they tell the story according to what they see. Writers cannot see the faces of their readers. They must first think about who their readers are. Then they must write with these readers in mind.

Writers must also think about their reason or purpose for writing.

Is it to make the audience laugh?

To make them understand?

To give them advice?

If writers remember their audience and purpose as they write, their readers will be able to better understand what is meant.

Three Compositions with Different Audiences and Purposes

The three samples of writing below show how one student wrote about the same experience but for different audiences and purposes. First, he wrote a letter to a friend back home. Then, he wrote a short composition for his English class. Finally, a year after the first two writings, he used the same event as part of an assignment for a college sociology class.

Letter to a Friend

Dear Ali,

I hope you are well and everything is OK in your high-school classes. I guess I'm OK, too. Remember when I promised to write you some letters in English? Well, here goes. I've got some advice for you, since you'll be coming to the United States next year.

Today I met an American family for the first time. Ya Salaam!* Did I make a big mistake! I was really proud of my English when I was being introduced to the family. I said things like, "I'm very pleased to meet you. How do you do." Things like that. When the mother showed me their new baby, a really cute little boy, I quickly thought of what I'd say in the village I grew up in and translated it into perfect English.

*Ya Salaam! is an exclamation in Arabic meaning Wow

"My, what an ugly baby!" I said. The mother looked at me kind of strangely. "Well, I think he's beautiful," she replied and turned her back on me. Nothing was quite right after that. When I got back to school and talked to one of the American teachers, she told me that in this culture, parents want to be told how pretty their baby is. It isn't bad luck to say this like it is in my village. What a lesson! So, my advice, Ali, is to learn more than grammar and writing. Try to learn about the culture from Americans or from people like me.

Time to study now. I'd better pen off. Write soon.

Your friend,
Khalid

Composition for Writing Class

Khalid's assignment for his English class was to "Tell about an experience from which you learned something about American culture."

A Lesson about Culture

Before I came to the United States, I thought I knew all there was to know about the English language. My first meeting with an American family, however, proved that I did not understand the connection between culture and language.

When I arrived at the home of my new friends, I was introduced to the children in the family. "I'm pleased to meet you," I said with a smile. I was very proud of the correct English I was using. Then the mother brought her youngest child into the room. "This is our new baby, Mark," she explained. She held the baby up for me to see. I responded by translating into perfect English what I would have said in the language of the village in which I grew up.

"My, what an ugly child!"

"What?" the mother said. "Did you say he's ugly?"

I knew then that I had done something culturally wrong. From that moment on I was determined to learn about the "do's" and "don'ts" of American culture in addition to studying English grammar.

Essay for Sociology Class

Khalid's assignment for his sociology class was: "Using your textbook in this class and your personal experience, explain the relationship between language and culture."

Language and Culture

Language and culture are inseparable. A language is like an index; it gives clues to what the people using that language value. From the index, one gets information about customs and beliefs, work, attitudes, family life, political institutions—and about the culture's past history. In other words, language reflects a culture.

All cultures have certain words that are taboo—words that should not be said in certain situations. In the traditional culture of my village, for example, people will look at a beautiful baby and say, "My, what an ugly thing!" They believe that to say the child is beautiful could bring harm to him or her. I realize this is just a superstition, but it is also a habit to respond this way. In the United States, on the other hand, a baby should be admired and her parents told how beautiful she is.

QUESTIONS FOR CLASS DISCUSSION

1. In the first example, the letter to Ali, who is the writer's audience? What is his purpose in writing to Ali? How would you describe the tone, or "feeling," of this letter? (Is it formal? Informal?) What kind of vocabulary does the writer use? Will Ali understand *ya salaam?*

2. In the second example, the composition, what differences do you notice in organization? Is there a clear thesis, or focus, sentence? Who is the audience? Why doesn't the writer use the Arabic words, *ya salaam?* What is the writer's purpose?

3. In the third example, the essay for sociology class, who is the writer's audience? What is his purpose in this writing? What differences do you notice—in organization, tone and vocabulary?

USING THE WRITING PROCESS TO IDENTIFY AUDIENCE AND PURPOSE

EXERCISE 3-1   Practice Writing with Audience and Purpose

In this exercise, you will be asked to put yourself "in the shoes" of an international student who has just bought a car and passed the driver's test for a state license. Although you do not yet have insurance, you decide to drive the car to school to show it to your friends. On your way to school you make an illegal right turn, going the wrong way on a one-way street. A driver coming from the other direction puts on his brakes but can't stop before hitting your car.

Read the details of the following police report and follow the instructions after it. Remember, you need to write for a different audience and purpose in each assignment.

Report of Motor Vehicle Accident

Driver and Owner Information

Name: Your Name   Date: April 20, 1988

License Plate No.: PKK886 1988 Colorado
Make of Vehicle: Toyota Celica, 2-door, 1985
Approximate Damage: $1,000
Description of Damage: Right front fender dented and turn signal light broken
Driver Comments: "I've never driven in this city before, and didn't know that I was turning onto a one-way street."

Charges: ILLEGAL TURN ON ONE-WAY STREET
         NO INSURANCE

Other Driver and Vehicle

Name: Eric Johnson

License Plate No.: RN1849 1988 Colorado
Make of Vehicle: Chevrolet King Kab, 1987
Approximate Damage: $1,500
Description of Damage: Left front fender dented, headlight smashed, hood damaged
Driver Comments: "I saw the Toyota turning the corner just in time to put on my brakes, but it was too late. I turned away but still hit the fender of his car."

Assignment 1

Using some of the information given in the police report, write a one- to two-paragraph letter to your father with the purpose of getting $2,500 to pay for damages to your car and to the car you hit. Choose details that will make your father understand your problem.

Assignment 2

Write a one- to two-paragraph composition for the members of your writing class. Your purpose is to give them advice about having insurance before they drive. Remember to use a thesis sentence. Use the story of the accident to support your thesis. Conclude by restating the thesis or by stating your advice to the students in class.

THE OTHER STEPS IN THE WRITING PROCESS

After you have looked over the **ideas** in the police report, **focused** on a thesis and **supported** it, read over your first draft. Ask yourself these questions:

Did I do what the assignment required? (Reread the instructions for each assignment.)

Did I have a clear focus in each composition? In other words, was there a good thesis statement that stated the topic and a controlling idea?

Did I support the thesis with the story of my experience?

Did I keep my audience and purpose in mind as I wrote each of the assignments?

Did I end the composition with a conclusion that fit my purpose in writing?

If you need to make changes in the organization of your composition, revise it and write it again. Remember to proofread and edit for spelling, grammar, and punctuation. Refer to the Editing Checklist at the end of the book.

THE FIVE *W*'S AND *H*

In Exercise 3-1, you used a small story, or an anecdote, to support your purpose in writing. When you wrote to your father, the story of the accident supported your purpose of getting money for damages. When you wrote advice to the class, the anecdote about the accident helped to support your advice that everyone who drives should have insurance.

An anecdote should give your readers the most important information about a happening. It should tell

Who was involved?

What happened?

Where did it happen?

When did it happen?

Why did it happen?

How did it happen?

EXERCISES TO POLISH UP YOUR WRITING

EXERCISE 3-2 **Important Questions**

Read the student composition that follows and answer the five *W* and *H* questions that follow to see if all the important information is included.

Sung Joo
Intermediate English
Professor Alvarez
November 2, 1988

Becoming Friends Again

When I was 10 years old, I started to play baseball. My best friend, Sang Do, also played on my team. One day during baseball practice, I had a fight with my friend. Although we were good friends, we did not speak to each other after that awful fight. Two weeks later, Sang Do wrote a composition in our writing class about the fight we had had. The teacher put all of the compositions on the board for the students to read.

When I read Sang Do's composition I found out that he had written the title, "Losing My Best Friend." In the composition, he said, "I made a big mistake. I want to ask my friend's pardon." Reading about our argument in his composition made me feel very sad, and it also made me hurry to his desk to apologize. We were reconciled and became good friends again.

1. **Who** is the story about?
2. **What** happens to the persons in the story?
3. **Why** do they have an argument?
4. **When** does the story happen?
5. **Where** does the story take place?
6. **How** is the problem solved?

You probably found that one of the questions above was not answered in the composition. Which one? Would it improve the composition if Sung Joo gave an answer for this question?

CHRONOLOGICAL ORDER

It is also important to use time words in an anecdote or in any composition that tells a story. These words help the reader to understand when events happen and in what order they happen.

Some Useful Words That Signify Time

first, second, third, etc.	after that
next	meanwhile
before	as
while	afterward
by that time	later
when, whenever	finally
after	from then on
soon after	during

EXERCISE 3-3   Time in a Narrative

Reread Sung Joo's composition, "Becoming Friends Again," and circle the time words.

EXERCISE 3-4   Ordering a Narrative Paragraph

Read the mixed-up sentences that follow. Decide the correct chronological order for these sentences. To make it easier, the sentence that should be first is numbered *1*. Place a *2* beside the sentence that should be next, a *3* beside the one after that, and so on.

"Yes" Means "No"

_____ I learned this lesson soon after I arrived in the United States. After I got off the plane, I was taken to the home of an American family.

_____ When my first day of English classes was finished, it was time to take the bus home.

_*1*_ One of the first lessons I learned in America was not to tell people I understand something when I do not.

_____ The next morning, the mother in my new family took me to school in her car.

_____ As we were driving to school, she asked, "Would you like to try taking the bus home after school, Taka?"

_____ While I was getting out of the car, I was very nervous and forgot where I had put the paper. I was nervous all during that first day at school.

_____ "Yes, yes," I said, although I had no idea where or how to take the bus.

_____ When we stopped in front of the school, my host mother showed me the bus stop and gave me a paper with the bus schedule and my new address and telephone number.

_____ "Yes, yes," I replied, trying to smile even though I understood very little of what she said.

_____ "Is everything OK, Taka? Do you understand what I just told you about the bus? Don't foget, it's the number 67 bus," she said, speaking slowly.

Share your answers with the class. Do you agree on the order? What are some of the time words that helped you to follow the order of events? Did the articles *a* and *the* help you to decide which action came first? (*a* paper . . . *the* paper)

Read the following paragraphs to see what happened next to Taka.

As I stepped on the first bus that came to the door of the school, I watched the person in front of me put two quarters in the box. I did the same.

"Can I help you?" the bus driver asked, noticing that I looked frightened. "Is this the bus you want?"

"Yes, OK" I replied.

While the bus was moving along the road, I looked for a familiar house or street but did not recognize anything. After 30 minutes, I still did not see the house of my American family. An hour later, the bus arrived at the airport where I had gotten off the plane the night before.

"Here's the airport. What airline do you want?" the driver asked.

"Yes, OK," I said and got off. Now where was I? What should I do? Where was the paper with my address and telephone number?

EXERCISE 3-5 **Finishing a Story**

What would you do if your were Taka? Finish this short story, or anecdote, with a paragraph that solves Taka's problem. Use some of the time words on page 54 to help the reader follow what Taka does. Use direct quotation for Taka's thoughts or for his conversation with other people. Don't forget to follow punctuation rules. Summarize the lesson Taka learned from this experience.

Direct Quotation

Hearing the actual words of a speaker makes a story more interesting. For example, when Taka says, "Yes, yes, OK," it seems more real than reading: Taka told the bus driver that it was OK.

The actual words of a speaker are called direct quotation.
When a writer tells his or her readers what a person has said,
this is called indirect quotation or reported speech.

Punctuation Rules for Using Quotations

The following rules will help you use direct quotation properly in your writing.

1. Use quotation marks (" ") at the beginning and end of the actual words spoken by each person. The name of the speaker and a word like *said* are outside the quotation marks.

> EXAMPLE
> "Here's the airport," he said.

2. Commas, periods, and question marks are put inside the quotation marks.

> EXAMPLE
> "Are you OK?" she asked.

3. In writing the words of more than one speaker, new quotation marks and a new paragraph are used every time the speaker changes.

> EXAMPLE
> "Thank you for helping me," Taka said quietly as he bowed to the old man.
> "You're certainly welcome," the old man replied.

EXERCISE 3-6 Changing Indirect to Direct Quotes

All the sentences that follow are indirect quotations. Rewrite these sentences as direct quotations, using the punctuation guide above.

1. Taka told the bus driver he wanted to go to Caley Street.

_____

_____

2. Taka told the man sitting next to him that he was from Japan. The man asked if he understood much English.

_____

_____

3. Taka told the man that he spoke just a little English. The man said he would help Taka get home safely.

_____

_____

4. Taka thanked the old man and smiled at him.

_____

_____

5. The old man told him good-bye and said he hoped to see him again.

_____

_____

COMBINING SENTENCES TO SHOW TIME RELATIONSHIPS

As you have learned in the previous exercises, writers of narratives must let their readers know **when** and **in what order** the actions in their stories take place. As you also have learned in the last chapter, writers need to **combine** short sentences into longer related ones. Both of these tasks can be accomplished by learning to use dependent clauses in your sentences.

> **Dependent clauses must always be attached to independent clauses. The dependent clause depends on the independent clause for its meaning.**
> **The kind of sentence that is formed by a dependent clause and an independent clause is called a complex sentence.**

For example, Taka said: "While the bus was moving along the road, I looked for a familiar house or street. . . . " *While the bus was moving along the road* is a dependent clause that states the less important, or subordinate, of two ideas. Putting these two ideas into one sentence that shows their relationship is better than writing two short, individual sentences, such as *The bus moved along the road. I looked for a familiar house or street.*

Adverbial Clauses

Dependent clauses are also called **adverbial clauses** because they work in the sentence just like an adverb, by describing a verb, adjective, or another adverb. Adverbial clauses also can change positions just as adverbs can.

EXAMPLE

> *While the bus was moving along the road,* I looked for a familiar house or street.

> While I looked for a familiar house or street, the bus was moving along the road.

To help you recognize and use dependent (adverb) clauses, here are some common **subordinating conjunctions** used to begin this type of clause. They are listed according to their type of relationship to the independent clause.

Time: after, before, since, until, as soon as, when, whenever, while

Place: where, wherever

Cause: because, as, as if, since

Purpose: so that, in order that

Result: so . . . that, such . . . that,

Condition: if, unless, provided that

Concession: although, even though, though, as long as

EXERCISE 3-7   Recognizing Dependent Clauses

All of the sentences in this exercise contain dependent clauses. Underline the dependent clause and circle the subordinating conjunction that begins the clause.

EXAMPLE

> I have not been ill (since) I came to this state.

1. When I first arrived in the United States, I was unable to speak more than a few words of English.

2. This was a very difficult experience because I love to talk to everyone I meet.

3. Whenever I would walk down the street in my own country, I would speak to the shopkeepers, the children, and the old people sitting on park benches.

4. I like living here although I get homesick sometimes.

5. While I am studying English, I also am trying to learn about American culture.

6. I will go to university provided that my English proficiency is high enough.

7. I will not go to the university until I have been home to visit my family.

8. I will be ready to study for four years after I have visited my family.

9. Before I choose the university that I want to attend, I must decide on my major field of study.

10. I will be very happy when I have made all these decisions.

EXERCISE 3-8   Combining Sentences with Dependent Clauses

In this exercise, combine sentences a. and b. into a single sentence. To do this, first decide which idea you will choose to make subordinate. Use this idea in the adverbial clause. Begin this clause with one of the words on page 60. Be sure to use a different word from this list for each sentence you write.

EXAMPLE
    a. My father died
    b. I came to the United States

    My father died after I came to the United States.
    or
    After I came to the United States, my father died.
    or
    Before I came to the United States, my father died.

1. a. I was lost.
   b. I was shaking and my stomach felt strange.

_____

2. a. I was pretending to listen to the teacher.
   b. I was really thinking of my vacation.

   _____

3. a. I arrived at John F. Kennedy Airport.
   b. I couldn't believe I was really in the United States.

   _____

4. a. I called my parents at home in Paris.
   b. I arrived at the hotel.

   _____

5. a. I claimed my luggage.
   b. I tried to find a taxi.

   _____

6. a. I slept quietly in my seat.
   b. I was traveling from Paris to New York.

   _____

7. a. I have been in the United States.
   b. I have been very busy.

   _____

8. a. The bus driver took my money.
   b. He asked where I was going.

   _____

9. a. I don't know something.
   b. I ask a question to find out.

   _____

10. a. I like it here very much.
    b. I am sometimes homesick.

    _____

Now check over your combined sentences. If the sentence begins with the dependent clause, put a comma after this clause.

EXAMPLE

When you need help, you must ask for it.

EXERCISE 3-9   **Writing an Anecdote about Yourself**

Taka, the student from Japan, wrote about his experience of getting lost. Have you, like Taka, had an interesting or funny experience in a new place? Write a one- to two-page anecdote about your experience, using the following steps.

1. Freewrite or list all the things you remember about this experience.

2. Number the events in the order they happened.

3. Use your freewriting or list to help you write a rough draft of your anecdote. As you write, try to use what you have learned about writing conversation and about combining sentences with dependent and independent clauses.

4. Share your rough draft with a classmate to get his or her suggestions. Ask your classmate these questions:

> Do you understand **who** the people are in my anecdote?
>
> Is it clear **what happened** and **in what order** the events happened?
>
> Is it clear **when** the events happened?
>
> Do you understand **where** the story took place?
>
> Is it clear **why** these events happened?
>
> Do you have any suggestions for making my story more interesting?

5. Use your classmate's answers to help you revise your anecdote.

6. Edit your composition for the errors you most often make in grammar, punctuation, and spelling. (See the Editing Checklist at the end of the book.)

7. Rewrite in the form suggested on pages 7-8.

8. After your instructor reads your composition, revise and edit it further if necessary.

MORE PRACTICE USING THE WRITING PROCESS

Legends and Folk Tales

In this chapter, you have practiced using small stories, or anecdotes, to support your ideas in a composition. Other important forms of story-telling are the legend and the folk tale. A **legend** is a popular story handed down from earlier times and a **folk tale** is a story from the common people of a culture that is told orally.

Legends and folk tales are a very important part of the national literature in most countries of the world. They are handed down by word of mouth from the old people to the younger ones. These stories tell the thoughts, feelings, beliefs, joys, dreams, and hopes of the culture in which they are born, but there also are certain common characteristics among all folk tales and legends. Many of them speak of the bravery of important men or women in the history of a country; some give us a picture of strange beings—talking turtles, dragons, magic birds. Other stories tell about the lives of kings, queens, and gods.

Folk tales and legends are fun to listen to, but they also teach us something about the meaning of life. There are folk tales about parents and children, about rulers of countries and the common people who serve them, about success and failure, and about love and hatred.

Can you remember one of the folk tales you were told as a child? Try to remember the details of the story.

The following is a folk tale written by a student from Nigeria.

Miriam Abouleye
Intermediate English
Professor Zucker
January 19, 1988

How Wisdom Was Scatterd Over the Earth to All Men

Mr. Tortoise was a smart and wise animal. Because of this, everyone sang about him when they played their drums.

Mr. Tortoise, son of Alika,
You are a clever person
Who digs in the earth
And finds a water fountain.

Mr. Tortoise told everyone how wise and clever he was, but when he was all alone he worried about losing his wisdom. He was afraid the other animals were jealous and might try to steal part of his wisdom.

He decided to put all of his knowledge, his special tricks, and his ideas into a gourd with a long neck and a big round belly. He then tied a string to the neck of the gourd and hung it around his own neck, so the gourd hung down on his chest. Then Mr. Tortoise found the tallest tree and, in the middle of the night, tried to climb to the very top. But each time he tried to climb the tree, the gourd got in his way and he fell down. All night long he tried.

In the early morning, Mr. Antelope came by.

"Good morning, Mr. Tortoise," he said. "What are you working so hard at this morning?"

"Hello, Mr. Antelope," answered the tortoise. "Thank you for asking. I have all my wisdom here inside this gourd. I plan to hang it up on top of this tree. My problem is how to get it there."

"That's easy," said Mr. Antelope. "All you have to do is put the gourd on your back. Then you can get a firm hold on the tree with no trouble. Once you get to the top, you can tie the gourd to a branch."

Mr. Tortoise did exactly what Mr. Antelope had suggested. When he reached the top of the tree, he realized that he wasn't as wise as he had thought. In fact, he knew now that the antelope was smarter than he. He was so disappointed in himself that he forgot about the gourd and let it fall to the ground where it broke into a thousand pieces.

That is how wisdom was scattered all over the world and why every man, woman, boy, and girl is able to pick up a little bit of it for themselves, but it is also why no one man has ever been able to learn all that there is to know.

GROUP ACTIVITY: TELLING FOLK TALES

Sit with a classmate and tell your classmate a folk tale from your country. Then have your listener ask questions to make sure the story was understood clearly. Next ask your classmate to retell your tale. You can help with details if he has difficulty telling your story.

After pairs of students have told and retold a folk story, the class may come together to discuss the different kinds of tales they have heard. The listener in each pair will report to the group, answering these questions:

1. What is the title of the folk tale?

2. What characters (people, animals, or things) are important to the story?

3. Is there a truth about life in the story? If so, what is that truth?

EXERCISE 3-10 **Writing a Folk Tale**

You have just gathered some ideas about folk tales from the countries represented in your class. Choose the tale you heard or told about or another one from your own culture. Record the tale in three to four paragraphs. Use specific words and phrases, the five *W*'s and *H,* and direct quotations when the characters in your tale speak. Conclude your folk tale with a statement of the truth that is learned in the story, if there is one.

EXERCISE 3-11   Help with Revising

After you have written the first draft of your folk tale, exchange it with a friend. Read each other's folk tales and answer these questions in writing.

1. Is the folk tale easy to understand?

2. Are there parts of the story that you have questions about? What are these questions?

3. Does the writer use some time words, so the story is easy to follow?

4. Does the writer use direct quotations to make the speakers seem real?

5. Does the writer end the story with a truth about life?

6. What do you like best about the folk tale?

7. What changes would you suggest, if any?

REVISION EXERCISES

REVISION EXERCISE 1   Following Suggestions for Revision

Read the following student composition. Use the suggestions that follow to rewrite the composition. Each sentence is numbered to help you. Do not correct grammar, spelling, or punctuation mistakes. You will do this in the next exercise.

Juan Carlos Garcia
Intermediate Writing
Professor Lenahan
January 6, 1987

(1)"Early to bed, early to rise, makes a man healthy, wealthy and wise." (2)This is an American saying. (3)I like it. (4)I wish I knew this saying when I was in the Venezuela. (5)When I was in my last year of secondary school, I worried. (6)I played too much instead studying. (7)I decide that I must study very hard before the final exams. (8)Every night I started study at 9 p.m. and study until about 5 a.m. (9)Then I fall asleep until 9 a.m. (10)I look at the clock. (11)Too late to go to school I say to myself. (12)So I go back to sleep until evening. (13)Then I start the studying again t 9 p.m. (14)I do this same way over and over. (15)Two weeks I do this. (16)My friend José say to me to come to classes because I was missing lectures. (17)I thought I know the answer.

(18)I did not listen to my friend. (19)Three days before the big exams I got sick. (20)The hospital say I have hepatitis. (21)They say I must rest for six weeks. (22)I could not take the exams. (23)I took them two months later and passed just a little.

1. Combine the first and second sentences.

2. Take out the third sentence because it is irrelevant.

3. Tell why the student wishes he had known the saying when he was in Venezuela. (sentence 4)

4. Combine sentences 4 and 5 to show the relationship between being worried and playing too much.

5. Combine "Then I fall asleep until 9 a.m." (sentence 9) and "I look at the clock" (sentence 10) with an adverb that shows the relationship in time.

6. Change what he says to himself to a direct quotation. (sentence 11)

7. Combine "I do this same way over and over" (sentence 14) and "Two weeks I do this." (sentence 15)

8. Change sentence 16 to a direct quotation that states the actual words José said to Juan Carlos.

9. Combine sentences 16 and 17 by adding a connecting word that shows contrast.

10. In sentence 20, change the word *hospital* to a more specific word.

11. Combine sentences 20 and 21.

12. Use a transition word in front of "I took." (sentence 23)

13. In sentence 23, "just a little" is out of order and it is incorrectly used. Can you think of a word or words that describe how Juan Carlos passed the exams? Place this word or words in front of the verb *passed.*

14. Write a concluding sentence that says something about the truth of the old American saying in sentence 1.

15. Write a title for the composition. Capitalize it correctly.

REVISION EXERCISE 2   **Following Suggestions for Editing**

Using the same composition, follow these instructions for changing grammar, punctuation, and spelling:

1. Change *knew* to the verb form that shows one action happening before another. (sentence 4)

2. Find the incorrect use of the article *(a, an, the)* in sentence 4 and correct it.

3. Change *I worried* to passive voice. (sentence 5)

4. Find the missing preposition in sentence 6.

5. *I decide* (sentence 7) doesn't agree with the verb tenses used in the rest of the composition. Change it to agree.

6. Add the missing word to *I started study.* (sentence 8)

7. Make *study* agree with other verb tenses. (sentence 8)

8. *Say* should also agree with other verb tenses. (sentence 11)

9. The word *way* is an incorrect usage. Change it to a more specific word. (sentence 14)

10. Check all the remaining verb tenses (sentences 12–23) to see if they agree in time with earlier verb tenses.

FOR WRITERS WHO HAVE MORE TO SAY

Journal Assignment

Write about an important lesson that was taught to you by your father or mother.

Class Assignment

1. Choose one of the following truths about life and explain it with an anecdote of one to two paragraphs.

> It is better to give than to receive.
>
> Talk is silver; silence is golden.
>
> One who has fallen into the water should not worry about getting one's clothes wet.
>
> A bird in the hand is worth two in the bush.
>
> The teeth are smiling but is the heart?

2. Turn a folk song into a folk tale. Think of a folk song from your culture. Use the events in the song as the actions in your story. The composition should be two to three paragraphs in length.

CHAPTER SUMMARY

A narrative is a story or description of events. Some form of the narrative can be used as support in many different kinds of writing.

One narrative form is the anecdote. An anecdote is a small story that tells about an interesting or funny incident.

A writer's audience are the people who read his or her composition. A writer must always think about the audience and the purpose of the composition, so that the readers will be interested in what is written and will be able to understand it clearly.

Conversation of characters in a narrative is made more real and interesting by the use of direct quotation rather than reported speech.

Time words are important in a narrative because they help the reader to understand when and in what order events happen.

Short sentences can be combined into longer, complex sentences by using dependent clauses. Dependent clauses also are called adverbial clauses. Time words sometimes introduce adverbial clauses.

CHAPTER **4**
Happy Families

All happy families are like one another.

—Leo Tolstoy

Family is defined as "parents and their children," or "persons related by blood or marriage; relatives; kinfolk," or finally, "all the members of a household; those who share one's domestic home."*

This definition tells us that a family might be as small as a mother and her children or as large as a group that includes parents, children, grandparents, aunts, uncles, and cousins. In addition, each culture has its own way of defining *family* and its size.

JOURNAL ASSIGNMENT

The photographs at the beginning of this chapter show two different families, one small and one large. All the family members in the photos seem to be happy and loving. As Tolstoy says, "All happy families are like one another." Do you agree? Do happy families, large or small, in whatever part of the world, share the same qualities? Write your thoughts about these questions in your journal.

DESCRIBING CHARACTERISTICS OF A PERSON OR GROUP

In this chapter you will use the theme of "family" to practice description in writing. Several kinds of college writing tasks require you to describe the characteristics of individual persons or groups of persons. A psychology professor might ask you to describe the actions of a person with a certain psychological problem or, in another situation, an instructor in a business management class might assign a paper on the qualities of a good manager. No matter what the assignment is, you can use the process of writing to describe characteristics.

USING THE WRITING PROCESS TO DESCRIBE

GROUP EXERCISE   Getting Ideas by Brainstorming

As you saw in Chapter 1, brainstorming is a quick method of getting many ideas from a group of writers. Study the photos of happy families at the beginning of this chapter. Think about the quote from Tolstoy, "All happy families are like one another." What ideas about happy families do the photos bring to your mind? What words describe a happy family in your culture? In the United States? Your instructor will write on the blackboard the words and phrases you suggest. Spend 5–10 minutes brainstorming. Try to think of at least 20 different ideas about happy families.

---

*"Family," *American Heritage Dictionary of the English Language*, 1981 ed.

Focusing

Look at the ideas that have been recorded on the blackboard. Are any of them related? (Lines can be drawn between those that are connected to each other.) What are the most important ideas in the list? (These may be circled.) What would you say are the major qualities of a happy family?

As a group, suggest several sentences that state your thoughts about happy families. These may be recorded on the blackboard with your ideas.

Of the sentences suggested on the board, which one best says what you think are the qualities of a happy family? Write this focus sentence here:

_____

_____

Gathering More Ideas about Your Focus

Now that you have a focus sentence, try freewriting for 10 minutes about this focus. You may wish to use your journal notebook for this writing. Write as quickly as you can without stopping to think about organization, grammar, punctuation, or spelling. You may be able to discover some new ideas about the topic if you keep your pencil moving. Use words in your own language if you can't think of them in English.

After you have finished freewriting, read through what you have recorded. If a reader only had time to read one sentence and not your whole piece of writing, what could you say about happy families in that one sentence that would tell your reader the most about your ideas? Write that one sentence here:

_____

_____

Supporting Your Main Idea in a First Draft

The sentence you just wrote should serve as a good main idea for one to two paragraphs about happy families. Support your main idea with other sentences that describe or give details about the main idea. Use the brainstorming ideas and your freewriting for support. Conclude your composition with a sentence that summarizes what you have said or restates your main idea in different words. Refer to the form of a Good Composition explained on page 7.

Getting Feedback on Your Writing

Read your first draft to a classmate. Ask your classmate to answer these questions:

Which part of the composition do you like best?

What is the main idea of the composition?

Do all the other sentences in the composition support this main idea?

Are there any places where you would like more explanation or more details?

Do the sentences seem to fit together smoothly? If not, in what places do ideas seem to jump from one to another?

Is the beginning of the composition interesting? Why or why not?

Does the conclusion "tie up" the ideas in the composition?

Revising and Drafting Again

Use your classmate's suggestions to revise your composition and draft it again. After you have written your second draft, ask the instructor for suggestions in editing mistakes in grammar, spelling, and punctuation. Also refer to your Editing Checklist at the end of the book. Then write the composition a final time, using the suggested form on page 7.

EXAMPLE OF A STUDENT COMPOSITION

Before you begin drafting your composition, you may wish to review the writing process by reading what Kritsana, a student from Thailand, wrote. To begin, with she did the following freewriting exercise. (Only the third, or last, draft has been corrected for grammar, spelling, and punctuation.)

Freewriting about "Happy Families"

Happy family. Not important to have money. Some student think money make happy family. I don't think so. How to make happy family depend on behavor, charcter, and choice. Family members must behave right way and have good charcter. Love is important, most important quality love and kindness. Also laughing, understanding, sympathy, forgiveness.

My family changed. In U.S. there is new happy family of mine. Andrew, Virachi, Adon, my three children like brothers and sisters. I have brothers and sisters in Chung Mai too. But now these friends are family of mine. It is really true family, we don't have to be relatives of blood—family. I mean we don't have to be conect by blood. We— instead—we work together, share, make family.

Focus Sentence: Important thing for a happy family is not money or relation by blood but love and sharing.

First Draft

Most important thing for a happy family is not money or relation by blood but love and sharing. How to make a happy family is depend on the peoples behavor, charcter and choice. But I think the most importand quality of a happy family is love and kindness, without them, life will be full of sorrow, jealousness and hopelessness. As we can find love, kindess, forgiveness, understanding, sympathy and laughter in a happy family.

Here in the United States we have formed a family. We are seven members together, four adults and three children of mine. Four of us are students at the college and we live as brothers and sisters, sharing our love and sorrow with each other. Our first member Andrew, who is 32 years old. He loves cooking. I'm the second, 28 years old, my husband was murdered about one and half years ago in Thailand. Because of my past misfortune, I came to the United States with my children and tried to forget my sorrowful past. Now we are in Colorado, my children are studying in elementary school. They enjoy their new life here. Next member is Virachi, who is 26 years old. He usually helps me take care of my children. Adon is the fourth member. He is 25 years old, loves to study, and brings a lot of funny things to make us laugh. Laughing and helping, we enjoy our life in Colorado.

Kritsana gave her first draft to a classmate to read. The classmate told her he really liked the part about the new members of her family. "Can you tell me more about each one?" he asked. Kritsana decided to include some more information about each person. When Kritsana asked her classmate for other suggestions, he said, "It ends so quickly. Maybe you can add something to the ending." Kritsana took these suggestions. She also decided to add a title and a few sentences of introduction about happy families in general. Then she wrote her second draft and gave it to her instructor for suggestions on how to correct grammar, punctuation, and spelling. (This draft is not included here.) Finally, she wrote her third draft.

Third Draft

Kritsana Udomsrirat
Intermediate Writing
Professor Ellison
April 6, 1988

My New Happy Family

Having a happy family is an important and precious part of everyone's life. Having happiness in a family does not depend on money or blood relationships. Instead it depends on the family members' behavior and character. I believe the most important quality of a happy family is love and sharing. Without these qualities, life would be full of sorrow, jealousy, and hopelessness. If a family loves and shares with each other, they will have other qualities, too, such as kindness, forgiveness, understanding, sympathy, and laughter.

Here in the United States seven of us have formed a happy family that shares and loves. We are seven members together, four adults and my three children. Four of us are students at the college and we live as brothers and sisters, sharing our happiness and sadness with each other. The oldest member is Andrew, who is 32 years old. Andrew is gentle and quiet, but he loves cooking. We always have delicious food to eat because of Andrew. I am the second oldest. Because my husband was murdered almost two years ago in Thailand, I came to the United States with my three children and tried to forget my sorrowful past. Now that we are in Colorado my children are studying in elementary school. They are pleased with their new life. The next oldest member of our family is Virachi, who is 26. He plays football very well and loves children, so he usually helps to entertain and take care of my children. Adon is the fourth member. He loves to study but is also quite talkative. Everyday after school we have funny news from Adon. He helps all of us to forget our homesickness.

Andrew, Virachi, Adon, my children, and I are not all blood relatives, but we are a very happy family that loves and shares in our new American life.

USING SPECIFIC WORDS

In the paragraph that you wrote about happy families, you should have used specific details and examples to make the reader see and understand what you mean by a happy family. Good descriptive writing, and all other types of writing, uses specific words and phrases. Interesting writing is specific writing. In the exercises that follow, you will have the chance to practice being specific in many types of writing tasks.

EXERCISES TO POLISH UP YOUR WRITING

EXERCISE 4-1   Using Specific Words and Phrases

On the left below there are sentences using general words to describe something. One or two words in each sentence are in italics. The italicized word or words, which are too general, should be changed to a more specific word or group of words. Read the examples shown for sentences 1 and 2; then complete the other sentences.

General	Specific
1. My family is *large*.	1. My family includes seven sisters and three brothers.
2. She is *very beautiful*.	2. She has long, black hair and sparkling brown eyes.
3. The house is *small*.	3. _____ _____
4. I don't know *much* English.	4. _____ _____
5. The history of my country is *very long*.	5. _____ _____
6. She finished English classes *quickly*.	6. _____ _____
7. Her grandmother is *quite old*.	7. _____ _____

8. The summer is *hot*.   8. _____

_____

9. I am tired from *working hard*.   9. _____

_____

10. I had *a lot of homework* last   10. _____
    night.

_____

USING SIMILES

Another way to make descriptive writing more specific is to use similes.

> **A simile is the comparison of two unlike things, using the word** ***like* or *as* to make the comparison.**

EXAMPLE
   The two brothers were *as* different *as* night and day.
   The last time I saw my grandmother, the skin on her face was *like* a dry, autumn leaf that clings to the tree.

The first simile compares "brothers" to "night and day," two very unlike things, but this comparison makes it very clear that the brothers are quite different from each other. The second simile compares an old woman's face to dry, autumn leaves. This comparison is good because it indicates the end of life: dryness, old age, wrinkles.

EXERCISE 4-2   Using Similies

Finish these sentences by adding similes. The first one is finished for you.

1. Living in a new culture is *like stepping off a moving train*.

2. Learning a second language is like _____

_____

3. Her blue eyes were as bright as _____

_____

4. The love of a husband and wife is as precious as _____

_____

5. The teenage dancers act like _____

_____

6. The angry football players hit each other like _____

_____

7. The circus acrobat flew through the air like _____

_____

8. My family is as important to me as _____

_____

9. Karim Abdul Jabar, the basketball player, is as tall as _____

_____

10. That policeman walking down the street looks like _____

_____

11. My airplane trip to the United States was as tiring as _____

_____

12. At 4 in the morning, my apartment is as quiet as _____

_____

13. Brooke Shields' smile is like _____

_____

14. Her sunburned face was as red as _____

_____

15. During the last snowstorm, my hands were like _____

_____

COMBINING SHORT SENTENCES

Descriptive writing often can be improved by combining short, simple sentences into longer ones that show relationships between ideas.

Read the two paragraphs that follow. The first mainly uses short, simple sentences. The second paragraph combines ideas into longer sentences

First Draft

My Family in the United States

We have formed a family here in the United States. It is very different from our real family at home in the United Arab Emirates. My new family includes four people. First is Ali. He is my oldest brother. He has become the "father." He helps us make decisions. He also gives us advice. Next is Mohamed. He was my best friend in high school. Mohamed is the cook. He also likes to clean house. The third person is Saleh. he is my cousin. He also is the dishwasher and the comedian. He wears an apron. Sometimes he puts on one of his silly hats. Sometimes he wears a cowboy hat or a baseball cap. He gets the dishes clean. He makes us laugh, too. I am the fourth member of the family. I don't like housework. I don't like to cook. I do like to study and to help my "family" with their college homework. As you can see, our "family" away from home works well together and keeps all of us from being lonely.

Second Draft

Faisal Maktoom
Intermediate English
Professor McNamara
June 28, 1988

My Life in the United States

Here in the United States we have formed a family that is very different from our real families at home in the United Arab Emirates.

My new family includes four people. First is Ali, my oldest brother, who has become the "father." He helps us to make decisions and gives us advice. Next is Mohamed, who was my best friend in high school. Mohamed cooks and cleans. The third person is Saleh, who is my cousin. Saleh is the dishwasher and the comedian. While he washes dishes, he wears an apron and one of his silly hats, either the baseball cap or the cowboy hat. Not only does he get the dishes clean, but he also makes us laugh. I am the fourth member of the "family." I also am a person who doesn't like housework and cooking. I do like to study and to help with the family's college homework. As you can see, our family away from home works well together and keeps all of us from being lonely.

Adjective Clauses

The style of the first paragraph is choppy because the reader must stop frequently. Ideas stand by themselves and are not related; hence, the reader must look back at the previous sentence to find a relationship. The second paragraph, however, reads more smoothly and has more variety in the length of its sentences. This paragraph, uses adjective clauses in many of the combined sentences.

> **An adjectival clause (sometimes called a relative clause) describes or limits a noun.**

Like the adverbial clause, discussed in Chapter 3, the adjectival clause is a dependent clause that cannot stand alone as a sentence because it makes no sense by itself. It must be connected to an independent clause. But unlike adverbial clauses, which can be placed at the beginning or end of a sentence, an adjectival clause can be placed only *after* the noun it describes, and it can never be placed at the beginning of a sentence.

The subordinators that introduce adjectival clauses include *who, whom, whose, that,* and *which.*

EXAMPLE

> Here in the United States we have formed a family *that is very different from our real family at home in the United Arab Emirates.*

Notice that the adjectival clause describes *family,* the word directly before the clause.

EXERCISE 4-3   Recognizing Adjectival Clauses

Find four sentences in Faisal's composition, in addition to the example above, that use adjectival clauses. Underline the clauses and tell which word each one describes.

Punctuation of Adjectival, or Relative, Clauses

There are two kinds of relative clauses: restrictive or nonrestrictive. The information in a restrictive clause is **necessary** to identify the noun phrase it describes or limits. Do not use a comma to separate the restrictive clause from the independent clause.

EXAMPLES

Restrictive: The two brothers *who are making dinner together* have prepared all the meals this month.

A body of land *that is surrounded on all sides by water* is called an island.

Nonrestrictive: The four students, *who live in an apartment near the college,* enjoy cooking meals together.

My family came from Malta, *which is an island in the Mediterranean Sea.*

A restrictive clause is **not** separated from the main clause by commas. A nonrestrictive clause **is separated** from the main clause by commas.

Bear in mind that *which* is used to refer to things only. *That* may be used to refer to both things and people. *Who* should be used to refer only to people and *whom* also is used for people but only when it is used as the object of the verb.

EXAMPLE

The new student *whom I met today* is from Africa.

EXERCISE 4-4   Combining Sentences by Using Adjectival Clauses

The sentences that follow describe the families in the photo at the beginning of this chapter. Use an adjectival clause beginning with one of these relative pronouns (*that, who, which,* or *whom*) to combine each group of short sentences. Place the idea you wish to emphasize in the independent clause and the less important idea in the dependent clause. Add commas to the nonrestrictive clauses.

EXAMPLE

    a. The husband and wife have only one child.
    b. The child is sitting near the mother.

    The husband and wife have only one child, who is sitting near the mother.

1. a. The mother is standing on the porch of her home in West Virginia.
  b. The mother has five young children.

    _____

2. a. The house has no electricity.
  b. The house is in a rural area of the state.

    _____

3. a. An electric washing machine is sitting on the porch.
  b. The washing machine was purchased from a neighbor.

    _____

4. a. All the children in the photograph are barefoot.
  b. This may mean they do not have shoes.

    _____

5. a. The mother must work very hard.
  b. The mother's children are posing for the photograph.

    _____

6. a. Her family is a very loving family.
  b. Her family includes seven persons.

    _____

7. a. Her family is happy in spite of the hardships they have suffered.
  b. Her family's income is very low.

    _____

8. a. The Chinese mother seems happy.
  b. She works beside her husband on the fishing boat.

    _____

9. a. The boat is very important to this family.
  b. This family uses the boat for fishing everyday.

    _____

10. a. The young Chinese boy looks sad or worried.
    b. The young boy is in the photograph.

    _____

11. a. The Chinese father speaks four different dialects.
    b. I really admire him.

    _____

12. a. We must look at the strengths of families.
    b. This is a better idea than looking at weaknesses.

    _____

EXERCISE 4-5   Polishing up Your Paragraph about families

Apply what you have practiced in the last three exercises to the paragraph you wrote about "Happy Families." Read over your paragraph to see if you can change any general words to more specific ones. Also look for one or two places where a simile might be appropriate. Lastly, check the paragraph for short simple sentences that might be combined into longer ones. If none of these suggestions fit your paragraph about "Happy Families," write a new paragraph that describes your own family and its members. Use specific adjectives and similes. Try to combine short sentences into longer ones that show relationships between ideas.

DESCRIBING PEOPLE, PLACES, AND THINGS

Thus far in this chapter you have practiced writing that describes qualities of a healthy, happy family. This type of writing requires a clear focus that is supported by specific words and phrases. In other types of assignments, you may be asked to physically describe persons, places, or things. Physical description is much like the description of qualities. It also requires a clear focus that is supported by specific words.

Here is a composition describing a place I often visited when in Cairo, Egypt.

Cleopatra's Perfumes

Even before I reached the open door on the west side of the shop called "Cleopatra's Perfumes," the sweet smell of jasmine, rose, and sandalwood tickled my nose. When I entered the dark shop through the clinking strings of beads covering the entrance, Ali, the manager, always invited me to sit on a soft, leather cushion next to a glass case filled with hundreds of little bottles of "essences," as he called them. Then Ali would slide the glass door to the right and take his most expensive "essence" from the top shelf of the case.

"This is perfect for you, madame," he would say while he removed the glass top from the bottle. Then he would firmly take my left wrist and touch the cold glass to it. "There, madame, wait a minute and then smell 'heaven'." I would wait, sniff the perfume, and be ready for the next fragrance, which would be dropped on my right wrist. Then Ali would sit down, sighing, on a cushion directly opposite my seat and tell me how bad business had been that week.

As you can see, good description uses many of the senses: sight, sound, smell, touch, and taste. Good description also makes clear the spatial relationships, or location, of the things being described.

EXERCISE 4-6   Using Descriptive Words

List the descriptive words you find in "Cleopatra's Perfumes" on the lines below.

1. Sight: _____

_____

2. Sound: _____

_____

3. Smell: _____

_____

4. Touch: _____

_____

5. Taste: _____

_____

6. Location: _____

_____

You may have noticed that there was no thesis statement in "Cleopatra's Perfumes"; in other words, there was no sentence that stated an attitude or opinion about the shop being described. Instead, the first sentence stated the *who, what, where,* and *how* of the topic. This sentence served the same purpose as a thesis statement. Another choice would have been to use a thesis, such as:

My sanctuary* in the middle of the crowded, noisy city of Cairo was a quiet, friendly shop that sold perfume.

FREEWRITING TO GET IDEAS

To help you remember details about your favorite place, spend five minutes describing everything you can recall about this place. On a separate sheet of paper write down anything that comes to mind. Keep your pen or pencil moving even if you have to write "I can't think of anything to say." Also if you can't remember a word in English, write it in your own language. You can look it up later in a dictionary.

At the end of five minutes, review your list. Can you think of any sense words to add to the list? Is there a special smell that you remember about the place? Are there sounds that you hear when you are in this place? When you are there, do you taste anything? How does it taste? Do you touch objects in the place? How do these objects feel? What are the most important objects (or persons) that you see in this place? Add these sense words to your freewriting exercise.

Next draw a map of this place, so that the location of important things will be clear to you.

Map of My Favorite Place

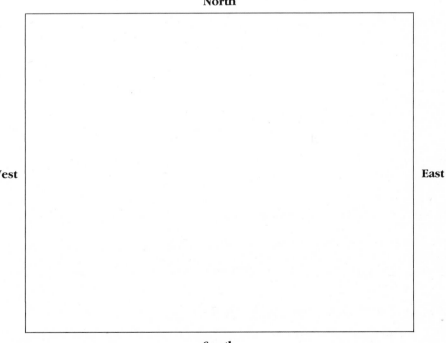

*A sanctuary is a protected place where a person is safe

FOCUSING

Look at the map you have drawn and your freewriting exercise. Ask yourself these questions: What is important about this place? Why is it important to me? What makes it my favorite place?

Write a thesis statement that tells your attitude, opinion, or idea about this place.

Thesis Statement: _____

_____

Using Sense Words

There are many words that you can use to refer to a particular sense. Listed below are just a few examples.

EXAMPLES

Sound: The ocean waves *slap, slosh, splash, kiss, caress,* the beach.
The wind *blows, whistles, breathes, whispers, sighs.*
The dishes *clatter, tinkle, crash.*

Taste: The food tastes *sour, sweet, salty, bland, spicy, peppery, hot, tart, bitter.*

Smell: The perfume smells *sweet, musky, spicy, fruity.*

Touch: The *cool* pillow feels *soft* and *smooth.*
The wet rock feels *slimy* and *slick.*
The sofa feels *rough* and *lumpy.*

Note: You may also wish to use similes to describe; for example, the sofa feels *like the back of a skinny old horse.*

EXERCISE 4-7   Using Sense Words

List the descriptive words from the sense word examples shown above and from your freewriting that support your thesis statement. Do you need to add other details that will "prove" your thesis statement to your readers?

EXERCISE 4-8   Describing Your Favorite Place

Write a composition of two to three paragraphs that describes your favorite place. Remember to use sense words and location words to paint a clear and interesting picture of the place.

You may use the thesis sentence in your first paragraph, following a more general introduction, or if you prefer, you may use it as the conclusion of your description. It is also possible to have an implied thesis statement, particularly in descriptive compositions. This means that the reader can tell what your main point is although it isn't expressed in the composition. Don't forget, however, that you must support the thesis (implied or not) with specific details.

Read aloud the first draft of the composition. Do you hear unclear ideas? Do you hear any mistakes in grammar or punctuation? Make necessary revisions and edit for mistakes.

EXERCISE 4-9   Reader Evaluation

Exchange your composition, "My Favorite Place," with that of a classmate. Read your classmate's composition and answer the following questions on the back of his composition.

1. What do I like most about the composition?

2. Did the writer do what the assignment asked; that is, did he describe a favorite place?

3. Did the writer include a thesis statement or imply a thesis? What is the thesis?

4. Do the details support the thesis?

5. Can I see the place? Are there words in the composition that help me to smell, touch, taste, and hear aspects of this place?

6. What suggestions do I have to improve the composition?

DESCRIBING A PERSON

Describing a person is much the same as describing a place. To allow the reader to "see" the person you are describing in the same way you "see" him or her, it is necessary to use specific details and descriptive adjectives and adverbs. It is also important to focus on the most interesting characteristic of that person. Is he very tall? Does she have a particularly bright smile? Are his eyes deep-set and mysterious? Your focus may be on the one feature of a person that a stranger would notice first.

EXERCISE 4-10   Describing a Person

Study the photograph of the retired silver miner at the beginning of the chapter, page 70. Then do the following.

List all the words or phrases that describe him.

Focus on one or two important characteristics, then circle all the words in your list that support this focus.

Write a main idea sentence that states your focus.

Now write a paragraph that describes this man, using your focus sentence and the circled words from your descriptive list.

Support the main idea with adjectives, similes, and specific details that describe.

Read the paragraph aloud to a classmate. Can your classmate visualize the old man from reading your description? Get feedback from your classmate.

Revise if necessary and draft the paragraph in the correct form.

REVISION EXERCISES

REVISION EXERCISE 1   Rewriting a Paragraph

Read this paragraph and follow instructions at the end to revise it.

My Necklace

My favorite possession is a small gold necklace. I left Mexico seven months ago and my boyfriend gave me this necklace when I left him at the airport. My parents and my two sisters also were at the airport to say good-bye to me. It was a very sad time, although I was happy to be traveling to the United States. The necklace has a chain with a locket. The locket has a nice shape. On the front of the locket there is a letter *N* for my name and some flowers. When I open the locket I see my boyfriend in it. He is really handsome. He has lovely hair and pretty eyes.

1. *Revise* the first sentence into a main idea that tells why the necklace is her favorite possession.

2. *Cross* out any sentences that do not directly support the main idea.

3. *Combine* sentences 5 and 6.

4. *Change* "nice shape" to more specific words.

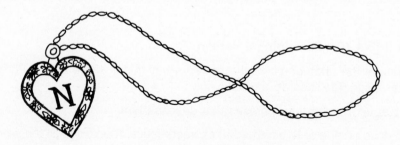

5. In sentence 8, the writer says she "sees her boyfriend" in the locket. Is this really true? Be more specific about where she sees her boyfriend.

6. Use more specific words to replace "lovely hair" and "pretty eyes." Combine these last two sentences.

7. Write a final sentence that concludes the paragraph.

REVISION EXERCISE 2   Adding Main Ideas to Paragraphs

Each of the following paragraphs is missing a main idea. After reading the paragraph, write a clear sentence that focuses on what is most important about the ideas in the paragraph. After you have written the main idea sentence, read the entire paragraph again. You may need to change a few words in other sentences to make your main idea fit smoothly.

A Good Language Teacher

_____

_____

The most important quality of a good language teacher is optimism. The teacher must believe that his or her students can and will learn the new language and must show this quality by offering encouragement to the students. The second quality is the ability to listen. A language teacher should plan activities that get students to speak while she listens. Thirdly, the good teacher should be well-trained in the techniques of teaching a language. Just being a native speaker of the language is not enough. These three qualities are essential if a teacher is going to help his or her students to learn effectively and efficiently.

My First Rodeo

_____

_____

Everywhere I looked there were cowboys in ten-gallon hats, boots, and old Levis. It was just like a scene from an old Western movie that I had watched back home. I fully expected to see one of the cowboys in a black hat pull out a gun and shoot a handsome cowboy in a white hat. Even the long-horned steers and bulls that I saw were just like the cattle in America a century ago. As I sat with the other spectators, I sniffed the close air around me: cigarette smoke, dry sawdust, and the strong smell of the animals. "All of these smells would be the same if I were watching a rodeo in the 1800s," I thought to myself. Then I took another sniff of the air. I smelled the bubbly cheese and tomato sauce of pizza, a food the cowboys of the past knew nothing about.

My Favorite Park Bench

_____

_____

The wooden bench was old and worn. All of the paint was gone and there were smooth places on the seat and the back from the generations of people who had rested there. I remember sitting on the bench with my grandmother when I was a child. She would tell me stories about the elves that lived in the park at night. Later, when I was a teenager, I got acquainted with a handsome young man on that same park bench. A few years after that, my future husband carved our initials on the back of the bench, "C. J. + M. L." This bench truly has been my friend for more than 30 years.

FOR WRITERS WHO HAVE MORE TO SAY

Journal Assignment

Pretend you can choose any place in the world for a vacation. Describe this "perfect" place in all the details you can imagine. What would you do while on this dream vacation?

Class Assignment

Choose one of the familiar objects from the list below. Describe the object in very specific words that detail its purpose, size, shape, color, and material, but do not use the name of the object in the paragraph that you write. Your writing should be clear enough that anyone reading your paragraph would be able to guess what the object is.

a push-button telephone   a small pocket comb
a typewriter   a car key
a piece of gum   a billfold
a can of Pepsi Cola   a credit card

CHAPTER SUMMARY

Description can be used in many types of writing. In this chapter, you have practiced describing a group (family), a place, a person, and, finally, an object.

Specific, definite words help the reader to see what you are describing. Description can also be made more alive by using words that involve the senses of taste, touch, smell, and sound.

Another way to add clarity to descriptive writing is to use similes. A simile is the comparison of two things that are unlike using the word *like* or *as*.

Descriptive writing can often be improved by combining short sentences into longer ones that show relationships between ideas. One way to do this is to use adjectival clauses that begin with *who, whom, which,* or *that*.

CHAPTER 5

Shadow and Sun

Shadow and sun—so too our lives are made.

—LeGallienne

"Shadow and sun—so too our lives are made" expresses a truth about life. This quote by LeGalliene is the theme of this chapter and is meant to encourage thoughts about the "shadow" and "sun" in your own life.

JOURNAL ASSIGNMENT

As you work through this chapter, keep the quotation in mind. Whenever you read or hear something that relates to the quotation, write about it in your journal. The notes in your journal are useful to you in two ways: you can learn more about yourself through these notes and you can get good ideas for additional writing in class.

USING THE WRITING PROCESS TO COMPARE AND CONTRAST

Each one of us goes through different stages of life. A person is born, grows up, and becomes an adult. Then each person arrives at middle age, grows old, and finally dies. These stages of life are called a life cycle. Each stage has its own difficulties and pleasures.

The photos and quotation at the beginning of this chapter say something about the stages of life. See how many ideas you can get by brainstorming a list of words and phrases with your classmates. As you may recall from other chapters, brainstorming simply means recording every idea that is suggested without stopping to discuss the ideas until the process is finished.

Study the photos. What words and phrases come to mind as you look at the pictures. Record all ideas on the blackboard. Spend no more than 5–10 minutes making the list of ideas. Remember, just think of as many words and phrases as possible; do not stop to discuss them.

NARROWING THE LIST OF IDEAS

Questions for Class Discussion

After brainstorming your list, try to answer these following questions. If the answers are included in your list of words, write the number of the question beside the answer. This task will help you to group your ideas.

1. In what stage of life are the man and woman in the first photo?

2. What words physically describe the couple?

3. Do their faces show how they feel about life? Can you describe this feeling?

4. How would you describe their house? How does this description fit the description of the old couple?

5. What season of the year is it in the photo? Is there a relationship between the season and the couple's stage in life?

6. What stages of life are the people in the other photo? What are the best descriptive words on the class list for these people?

7. How does the quotation from LeGalliene fit your ideas?

FOCUSING

Your discussion of the stages of life probably has given you many ideas. Try to focus or organize these ideas by classifying life into its major stages, starting with birth and ending with death.

To see these stages more clearly, draw a time line of them like the one shown below. You may divide the stages into age groupings that are important in your culture. Below the line, list any difficulties or bad points of the age. Above the line, list the pleasures or good points of the age. To get you started, several ideas have been placed on a sample Life Stages Diagram. After diagramming the stages of life and their good and bad points, you may wish to share your ideas with the class.

Read over the brainstorming list and review the diagram you made of the stages of life. What have you discovered about life's stages? Spend several minutes writing down these important ideas.

Now decide which of the "discoveries" about life you would like to use as the topic of a short (two- to three-paragraph) composition? You are ready to make a plan for an essay and to decide on some guidelines to help you.

Purpose
First, you need to decide on a purpose for writing about your topic. The following list suggests some purposes. Choose one of them and make it fit your topic.

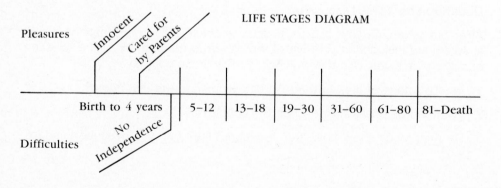

My purpose is to:

give my readers information about _____

explain to my readers why _____

make my readers believe that _____

describe _____ to show my readers_____

_____

compare _____ with _____ to show my readers_____

_____

state an opinion about _____ and show my readers why I have that

opinion

analyze _____ into (how many?) _____ parts to show my readers__

_____

Guideline Sentences

My purpose in writing is to_____

_____

The main point I want my readers to understand is_____

_____

SUPPORTING

Now, following the two guideline sentences you have just written, make a plan for your first draft by listing the supporting points you will use to develop the main point you have stated in your second guideline sentence.

Your supporting sentences should give specific examples, details, description, or explanation of the main point.

The following plan was made by Mitsuo, a Japanese student:

My purpose is to analyze life's stages into six parts and to explain to my readers which stage is the foundation of my future life.

The main point I want to get across to my readers is that the young adult stage I am in right now is building the foundation of my future.
Supporting Points:

1. *Six stages of life and their advantages*
   baby: innocent, cared for
   childhood: learning new things
   adolescence: unstable but beautiful
   young adult: independence, education, marriage, job
   middle age: place in society
   old age: heroic respect

2. *My stage —young adult*
   college
   job
   travel
   new friends
   marriage and baby
   success and failure

Now write your own plan on a separate sheet of paper.

DRAFTING

Now you are ready to write. Keep your purpose in mind and use your main point as the thesis of your essay. Use your plan to guide your writing. Remember that good writers, even professional ones, do not produce perfect essays the first time. They have to rework ideas, write many drafts and make numerous changes. If you find that you need to change your plan because other ideas develop, feel free to do so. Being the writer means that you can change the direction of your writing whenever you choose. You can throw out an idea and start again.

Here is Mitsuo's first draft:

First Draft

The Stage of Life

Life can be divided into six stages. The first is a babystage; Babies are cared for by their parents and are innocent. The second stage is childhood; the children are also cared by parents, but they are interested in everything and learn it. The third stage is adolescence, which is a beautiful stage because they come to know love and manage their lives. Early adulthood is a time when they came to be independent from their parents, so they have many experiences: higher education, getting a job, marriage and building their family. The next stage is middle age. This is a time when their place in society is established. They come to be complete and have the most responsibility in their life. The last age is old age which is a heroic age. They should be respected by the people of other life stages because they are wiser and have more experience.

I have thought through own my stage of life. Now, I have begun to climb the stage of middle age. I'm satisfied with my last stage: the young adult stage. After I graduated from the college, Nagoya Institute of Technology, I have worked for Toshiba for 11 years. I had many experiences and education in this term. I have been to many places, not only Japan but also Europe. I have had many friends and a new family. I had many successes and failures in my job. This stage had a strong contrast—like sun and shadow. It is the foundation of my future life. My work will be harder and harder with many interesting experiences. My responsibility will be bigger in my family and my social life. I hope that I will be able to be satisfied with my last stage when the next stages comes, until old age.

REVISING

In most of the compositions you have written before, you were asked to have a classmate read them and give you feedback. It is also important for a writer to learn how to read his or her own work in order to make changes.

Read your composition aloud and then ask yourself these questions:

1. Have I clearly stated a thesis that expresses the most important idea?

2. Does all the information in this draft relate directly to my thesis?

3. Are there any places in the composition where I need more explanation, examples, or details?

4. Are there places where I jumped from one idea to another?

5. Do I have an introduction that gets the reader's attention?

6. Do I have a conclusion that summarizes or restates the thesis in a new way?

When Mitsuo read aloud his composition, he decided that he really had not stated a thesis for his entire composition; instead he had a main idea for each paragraph. He decided it would be better to let the reader know at the beginning what focus he had chosen for his composition. Thus, he worked hard to write a thesis statement. Mitsuo also found a few places where he seemed to jump from one idea to another. He added some transitions to make connections between these ideas. Finally, he added a conclusion to "tie up" and complete his composition.

Mitsuo's Second Draft

Mitsuo Nakamura
Intermediate Writing
Professor Torelli
September 21, 1988

The Stage of Life

Although life can be divided into several stages, each with its own characteristics, the stages are not equally important. It is my opinion that the fourth stage, early adulthood is the most important part of my life. Although this is true for my life, another stage may be more important for other persons.

What are the stages of life? Life can be divided into six stages. The first is a babystage; babies are cared for by their parents and are innocent. The second stage is childhood; the children are also cared by parents, but children are interested in everything and learn very quickly. The third stage is adolescence, which is a beautiful but unstable stage because they come to know love and to manage their lives. Early adulthood is a time when human beings come to be independent from their parents, so they have many experiences: higher education, getting a job, marriage, and building a family. The next stage is middle age. This is a time when men and women establish their place in society and have the most responsibility. The last age is old age, which is a heroic age when human beings should be respected by the people of other life stages because they are wiser and have more experience.

In thinking through my own stage of life, I have found that I am just leaving a very important stage, the young adult stage. After I graduated from college, Nagoya Institute of Technology, I have worked for Toshiba for 11 years. I had many experiences and education in this term. I have been in many places, not only Japan but also Europe. I have had many friends and a new family. I had many successes and failures in my job. This stage had a strong contrast—like sun and shadow, but I am very satisfied with what has happened in my young adulthood. It is the foundation of my future life. My work will be harder and harder with many interesting experiences. In addition, my responsibilities will be greater in my family and my social life. In spite of all the difficult things I face in middle age, I think I will succeed because I have built a strong foundation in young adulthood, the most important stage in my life.

Let your answers to the revision questions on page 99 guide you in making changes in your composition. Also refer to your editing checklist at the end of the book. Then edit your essay for grammar, spelling, and punctuation. Draft it in final form and submit it to your instructor, who will make further suggestions for improvement. Mitsuo, for example, wrote a third draft that included a change in his title ("The Most Important Stage in My Life"), some changes in vocabulary, and correction of verb tense and punctuation mistakes.

POLISHING YOUR WRITING

Using the Colon

When you express your ideas in a classification form, you often use the colon (:) to introduce a list of groups or categories. The colon is used **only after nouns** that tell the category, never after verbs or prepositions.

EXAMPLES
Life can be divided into five stages: childhood, adolescence, early adulthood, middle age, and old age.
Childhood has three major advantages: being cared for by someone else, few responsibilities, and the opportunity to grow and develop.
The students in my class include Japanese, Koreans, Arabs, and Latin Americans.

Notice that there is no colon in the last example because *include* is a verb.

Colons are not used after verbs. Also notice that each item in a series of three or more is followed by a comma, (Japanese, Koreans, Arabs, and Latin Americans.)

EXERCISE 5-1   Using the Colon

Punctuate the following sentences. Use a colon where necessary and place commas between items in a series.

EXAMPLES
  There are three primary colors: red, blue, and yellow.
  The primary colors are red, blue, and yellow.

1. There are two basic types of vegetables those that grow aboveground and those that grow underground.

2. We can categorize higher education in the United States into three divisions community college college and university.

3. Major food groups are milk fruits vegetables fats and grains.

4. The United States is divided into 50 states.

5. Microscopes are classified according to the type of lens simple compound or electron.

6. English language study usually is categorized into subject areas grammar writing reading and listening/speaking.

7. Major team sports in the United States are football baseball basketball soccer softball and volleyball.

8. Team sports and individual sports are the two major groups, depending upon how many players participate.

9. According to size and body style, there are five models of automobiles coupe sedan station wagon limousine and convertible.

10. Major airlines that use our airport are United TWA Continental and Northwestern.

Using a Variety of Classification Terms

When you write a classification composition, it is more interesting to use different terms rather than repeating the same one.

Helpful Classification Terms

We can/ may/ might divide _____ into _____.
            classify
            categorize
            group

_____ can/ may/might be   divided into _____.
                                                 classified into
                                                 categorized into
                                                 grouped into

There are _____ classes of _____.
                                            kinds of
                                            methods of
                                            categories of
                                            groups of
                                            divisions of
                                            qualities of

EXERCISE 5-2 **Practice Writing Classification Sentences**

Write a sentence classifying each of the following items into categories. Use the same sentence pattern (see Helpful Classification Terms above) only once.

EXAMPLE
  Magazines

      Magazines can be classified into three types: weekly, monthly, and quarterly.

1. Students in your class

   _____

2. Sports in your country

   _____

3. Jewelry worn by women

   _____

4. Newspapers

   _____

5. Higher education in your country

   _____

6. Foods that are your favorites

   _____

7. Chapters in this book

_____

8. Pets

_____

9. Makes of automobiles popular in your country

_____

10. Languages spoken in your country

_____

EXERCISE 5-3 Writing a Classification Composition from Facts

Many of your college and university classes will require you to write compositions using statistics as support. This exercise will give you practice in using facts in your writing.

Estimated Religious Population of the World*

Statistics of the world's religions are only rough approximations. Aside from Christianity, few religions, if any, try to keep statistical records. The compiling of statistics is also complicated by the fact that in China one may be at the same time a Confucian, a Taoist, and a Buddhist. In Japan, one may be a Buddhist and a Shintoist.

Estimated Religious Population of the World

Source: the 1986 Encyclopaedia Britannica Book of the Year

Religion	N. America[1]	S. America	Europe[2]	Asia[3]	Africa	Oceania[4]	Totals
Total Christian	262,870,400	195,431,000	329,380,000	106,230,000	149,200,200	18,600,000	1,061,711,600
Roman Catholic	143,850,000	165,100,200	177,140,200	58,100,200	59,700,000	5,100,200	628,990,900
Eastern Orthodox	5,320,400	330,400	43,430,300	2,800,000	6,700,200	370,000	56,951,100
Protestant[5]	113,700,000	10,000,400	108,809,500	45,329,800	82,800,100	13,129,800	373,769,600
Jewish	7,630,000	720,200	3,800,100	4,480,200	227,500	74,000	16,932,000
Moslem[6]	1,820,000	390,100	20,400,000	361,700,800	150,300,000	89,000	554,700,200
Zoroastrian	2,700	2,600	14,000	230,000	1,500	—	250,800
Shinto	48,000	—	—	32,000,000	—	—	32,048,000
Taoist	30,000	11,000	12,000	20,000,000	—	3,000	20,056,000
Confucian	100,000	56,000	410,000	150,400,000		18,000	150,984,000
Buddhist	350,200	248,000	210,000	246,740,300	15,000	24,000	247,587,500
Hindu	380,000	615,200	390,000	461,300,000	800,000	325,000	463,815,200
Totals	273,231,600	197,474,100	354,616,100	1,403,081,300	300,544,200	19,138,000	2,548,085,200
Population[7]	400,802,000	268,825,000	775,310,000	2,819,061,000	553,210,000	24,820,000	4,842,048,000

The World Almanac and Book of Facts, 1986 ed., © Newspaper Enterprise Assn., Inc., 1986, N.Y., p. 79.

Questions for Class Discussion

1. What religion has the most members in the world?

2. What religion is second in world numbers?

3. What religion is third?

4. What religion is fourth in membership?

5. How does the population of a world area relate to the number of religious members?

6. Read the paragraph under the title, "Estimated Religious Population of the World." What are some of the problems in comparing the numbers of members in these religions?

Study the statistics; then write a paragraph that classifies the four major world religions by numbers of members.

Begin with a main idea (statement of classification).

Support this idea with sentences that give the statistics for each religion.

Conclude with a sentence that generally states the problem of keeping records of members.

Remember to revise and draft again if there are changes that need to be made in your paragraph.

The next two exercises—Outlining and Sentence Combining—will help you to write the paragraph.

OUTLINING A COMPOSITION

An outline is a formal division of a paragraph or a composition into groups of ideas.

The formal outline uses Roman numerals (I, II, III, IV, V, and so on) for major groups and capital letters (A, B, C, D, and so on) for subgroups.

Outlines are helpful either in planning a composition or in checking to see if it is well organized after you have written the rough draft.

EXERCISE 5-4   Outlining a Composition

Using the statistics from the chart of religions, plan a five-paragraph composition on the general topic "Major Religions of the World." Some of the divisions have already been filled in. Fill in the blanks for the remaining ones.

Title: _____

Thesis:

   Major religions of the world, according to numbers of members, include
      Christian, Moslem, Hindu, and Buddhist.

   I. Christian
      A. World members—1,061,711,600
      B. North America—largest membership

  II. _____

      A. _____

      B. _____

 III. _____

      A. _____

      B. _____

  IV. _____

      A. _____

      B. _____

   V. Difficulty in Getting Statistics

      A. _____

      B. _____

COMBINING SENTENCES

In Chapter 4, you combined short sentences into longer, complex ones by using
adjectival clauses that begin with words such as *who, whom, which,* or *that.* The
following exercise will give you additional practice in sentence combining. Because
these sentences deal with things or concepts, rather than people, you will use the
relative pronoun *which* to begin the clause.

EXAMPLE

   Christianity is one of the major world religions. Christianity includes Roman
      Catholic, Eastern Orthodox, and Protestant divisions.

Combined: Christianity, *which includes Roman Catholic, Eastern Orthodox, and Protestant divisions,* is one of the major religions of the world.

In sentences like these, the least important information is put in the *which* clause. What is the most important information in the combined example above? The least important? It is also very important to note that the *which* clause is placed directly after the word it describes.

EXERCISE 5-5 Using *Which* to Combine Sentences

Using *which,* combine each group of sentences into one complex sentence. The first five sentences are easier; the remainder are more difficult.

1. My class has more than six different nationalities.
   My class is advanced reading.

   _____

2. Saudi Arabia has both mountains and deserts.
   Saudi Arabia is located on the Arab Gulf.

   _____

3. I am from Thailand.
   Thailand used to be known as Siam.

   _____

4. This ring has been in my family for more than 100 years.
   This ring was given to me by my grandmother.

   _____

5. Sociology is a very difficult subject for me.
   Sociology is a five-credit class.

   _____

6. The Moslem religion has the most members in Asia.
   The Moslem religion numbers more than 555 million people.

   _____

7. The smallest number of Moslems is in Oceania.
   Oceania includes Australia and New Zealand.

   _____

8. The greatest number of Hindus are found in Asia.
   Asia, of course, includes the country India.

   _____

9. North America has 336,000 Buddhists.
   North America also includes more than a million and a half Moslems.

   _____

10. The Zoroastrian religion is not very well known.
    The Zoroastrian religion was started in Persia in the sixth century.

    _____

COHERENCE: A QUALITY OF GOOD WRITING

The word *coherence* means connected, united, logically ordered. Coherence is a very important quality of good writing. All the sentences in a paragraph and all the paragraphs in a composition should be connected in a smooth, logical way. It is very important that the reader of your writing be able to understand the connection between one thought and another. If your writing is not coherent, the reader will be unable to follow your ideas easily. In fact, the reader may decide *not* to read writing that is incoherent.

What Makes Writing Coherent?

The first requirement of coherent writing is a well-organized composition. It should have a clear thesis, supporting paragraphs, each of which has a main idea (topic sentence) related to the thesis, and a strong conclusion.

The second requirement of coherent writing is that ideas within a paragraph should flow smoothly. This can be done in one or more of the following ways:

Using pronouns

When a pronoun in a sentence refers to a word in a previous sentence, the two sentences will "stick together."

EXAMPLE
   Pollution is a major health problem in this city. *It* is the result of automobile exhaust fumes.

Repeating key words and phrases

Repeating words within a paragraph, especially the controlling ideas in the topic sentences, will make your paragraph seem smoother. Using synonyms for these words and phrases also adds coherence.

EXAMPLE

Studying English can provide the *key* to higher education for students from non-English speaking countries. This *key* can open the door to college and university degrees in fields that are needed to develop many nations of the world.

Using linking words and phrases

These words and phrases connect ideas within a paragraph and help to carry ideas forward from one paragraph to another. In other words, they provide transitions between ideas.

Here is an example of transitions within a paragraph. The linking words and phrases are in italies.

The dinner menu in a medium-priced American restaurant usually is divided into four sections. *First of all,* it mentions appetizers, which include before-dinner dishes, such as shrimp cocktail. *Second,* there is the section that lists different types of salads. *The third one* is the longer list of entrees, or main dishes. *Finally,* desserts are listed. *In addition* to these four sections, some menus list beverages separately.

An example of transitions between paragraphs can be seen as the composition on menus is continued:

On the other hand, dinner menus in expensive restaurants may contain as many as seven or eight different sections. . . .

In this example, the phrase *on the other hand* signals a transition from talking about menus in medium-priced restaurants to those in expensive restaurants. When a reader sees a phrase such as this, he or she prepares for a contrast in ideas.

Some examples of linking words and phrases are listed below according to the relationship between ideas that they show:

Space or Position		Time	
on the right of	next to	first, second, etc.	later
parallel to	below	next	after
beside		before	finally
		while	meanwhile

Similarity		Contrast	
like, likewise		but	still
at the same time		though	although
once again		however	on the other hand
		yet	

Addition		Result	
and		because	consequently
in addition		as a result	therefore
also			
furthermore			

Conclusion or Summary
in conclusion   in a word
in summary   finally

EXERCISE 5-6   Recognizing Words and Phrases that Make Coherent Writing

The first step in learning to use words that add coherence to your writing is to recognize them. The composition that follows contains both pronouns that refer back to nouns and linking words and phrases that provide transitions between ideas.

First, circle the linking words and phrases. Then go back and underline each pronoun that refers back to a noun. Read the essay a third time and underline twice each of the key words that is repeated.

EXAMPLE

Good language learners have three major characteristics. First, they must have an "ear" for the music of the language.

English Spoken Here

More people in the world speak English than any other language. In fact, 345 million people use English as their first language and an additional 400 million speak it as their second. English is the native language of 12 countries and an official or semiofficial tongue in 33 others where it is used to conduct at least some government business. Furthermore, it is a subject studied in the schools of another 56 countries.

Although English is a popular language, it is not an easy one. Learners of English struggle over irregular verbs, strange idioms, and crazy spellings. Why? Because they see English as the language of success and of status. For example, in Japan a recent newspaper ad offered an extremely good salary to any Japanese who could write technical manuals in simple English. In addition, a knowledge of informal phrases is particularly valuable in that country. Some years ago, Sony corporation placed this ad: "Wanted: Japanese who can swear* in English."

*To use impolite words, such as *damn, hell,* etc.

EXERCISE 5-7 Choosing Linking Words and Phrases

The following paragraphs use several linking words for coherence. Circle the correct word or words from those listed in the parentheses.

Sounds Become Words

Some language experts believe that early people tried to make words by imitating the sounds of nature and of the animals around them. (But, In fact, While), some of these words continue to be part of our languages today. (And, For example, As a result) the word for the sound we make when we sneeze is *atchoo* in English, *atchis* in Spanish, *atchouin* in French, and *hatschi* in German. (As you can see, Because), the words above are very much alike, probably because these languages are related. (As a matter of fact, However,) the Japanese word for the sneeze sound is *gu-gu* and the Indonesian word is *wahing*. These examples prove that people all over the world do not say things in the same way.

(In addition, First, Yet,) language experts believe that the first full words in the world were teaching words like "Run!" "Cut!" "Push!" "Pull!" although, of course, they were not in the English language. Teaching words are action words, (meanwhile, in conclusion, of course). Prehistoric people used them to tell each other what to do.

REVISION EXERCISES

REVISION EXERCISE 1 Adding Linking Words and Phrases

Add linking words and phrases to make a smooth, flowing paragraph. Write the words and phrases in the blanks provided. Also add pronouns that refer back to nouns.

Children's TV Can Be Good

Children should be encouraged to watch only those television programs that will make their lives better, according to Vance Packard, media researcher and author. Four types of television programs are suggested by

Packard. _____ are programs that involve exploration or

experiments. _____ ''Mr. Wizard'' uses everyday objects

to help children understand the basic ideas of science.

_____ are shows that activate imagination, such as Charlie

Brown specials, Jim Henson's Muppet characters, and the Disney chan-

nel. _____ includes programs in which adults and children

are shown doing things together. When children watch programs such as

_____, _____ see that they are not isolat-

ed from adults. The fourth type are programs that make young people

think about the social problems of growing up or about conditions in the

world. _____, ''CBS News Sunday Morning'' and similar

programs give children a good understanding of the world and

_____ problems.

REVISION EXERCISE 2 **Completing a First Draft**

Read the incomplete rough draft below and follow the instructions after it.

Our school is like a miniature United Nations because it includes representatives from all over the world. The 98 students and teachers can be classified according to the continents from which they come.

Asia—45 students

Europe—10 students

Africa—12 students

North America—18 teachers

South America—18 students

Australia—1 teacher

1. Write sentences to support the main idea. Use the notes given by the student. Use linking words wherever possible.

2. Write a concluding sentence.

3. Write a title.

4. Copy the entire paragraph in correct form.

FOR WRITERS WHO HAVE MORE TO SAY

Journal Assignment

Write about the "sunniest" days of your life. Write about those days that were filled with "shadows."

Class Assignment

Each of the following assignments involves observation of persons and events around you and the classification of these.

1. Discuss the types of people you see in a shopping mall.

2. Discuss the types of behavior of students in the cafeteria.

3. Discuss the types of popular music and the age groups to which each type appeals.

4. Discuss the various styles of dress of students in your school.

5. Discuss the types of teachers or teaching styles in your school.

6. Discuss the types of food most popular in your country.

CHAPTER SUMMARY

Classification is a way of organizing your ideas. You have practiced using classification in a composition focused on your own experience and in other writing that focused on facts.

The colon (:) is frequently used in sentences that classify. The colon introduces a series of items or groups.

An outline is a formal division of a paragraph or a composition into groups of ideas. Outlines are helpful either in planning a composition or in checking to see if it is well organized after you have written the rough draft.

Coherence, which means clearly connected ideas, is an important quality of writing. Three ways of achieving coherence include the following:

repetition of key words and phrases

using pronouns that refer back to nouns

using linking words and phrases.

CHAPTER 6

The Ways of Your Ancestors

The ways of your ancestors are good. They cannot be blown away by the winds because their roots reach deep into the soil.

—Okot P'Bitek

"The ways of your ancestors" are the traditions of your culture that have been passed down through generations of people. The "roots" of these traditions may go back hundreds, even thousands, of years. But, in spite of the deep roots, traditions can change. Sometimes traditions of the past are reshaped to meet the different needs of the present. Sometimes they are changed simply because they do not seem appropriate to modern times.

In this chapter, you will discuss some traditional parts of American culture and of your own culture, and you will compare and contrast these traditions in writing.

JOURNAL ASSIGNMENT

What are some traditions of your own family that you hope to pass on to your children?

USING THE WRITING PROCESS TO COMPARE AND CONTRAST

When your purpose in writing is to show the similarities and differences between two things, you use comparison and contrast. The contrast in how things look usually draws attention most quickly. For example, when you look at the photo of a Nigerian street at the beginning of this chapter, what do you notice first? Is the Coca-Cola sign surprising? To what is the sign a contrast?

Getting Ideas by Listing

Divide into groups of three students each for this exercise. Assign one person to record the group's ideas. On a piece of paper, the recorder should make two columns, one labeled "Old" (traditional) and the other "New" (modern). Study the photos that appear at the beginning of the chapter and list as many traditional things as you can see. Then make a list of the modern things in the photos.

After you have spent a few minutes making your list, add to it by guessing at other traditional aspects not shown in these photos of the two countries (Nigeria and Kenya). Do the same for modern aspects that don't appear in the photos.

Now study the list. Can any of the items be grouped together? For example, bicycles and cars might be grouped as transportation. Draw lines between similar items and label them with the general group in which they fall.

Each group should share its list with the class.

Focusing as a Class

When you study the lists and look at the pictures, what general ideas do you get about the traditional and the modern aspects of countries like Nigeria or Kenya?

Put these two ideas into sentence form below.

Focus Statement: _____

_____.

Focus Statement: _____

_____.

Do either of the focus statements above fit your native country?

EXERCISE 6-1 **More Ideas**

Since you know more about your own country than you do about the countries in the photos, make a similar list on a separate sheet of paper of traditional and modern aspects of your native country. Remember to consider specific things in areas such as family life, roles of men and women, social life, business, religion, education, industry, etc. Be specific.

Look back over your list and draw connecting lines between any aspects that go together. Label these with more general headings, such as those above. For example:

Traditional	Modern
Behavior of Older People	*Industry*
Older women wear tradition-al clothing	Auto factory, Computers
Old people still go to church	Light industry, shoes, clothes
Hand-made things are sold to other countries.	
	Social Life of Young People
Grandparents live with their family.	Teens in cities date
	Discos, movies

EXERCISE 6-2 **Focusing**

Now go back over the list and answer each of the following questions in a complete sentence.

1. Are there more traditional aspects in your country than modern ones? Or the opposite?

    My country has more _____

    _____.

2. Are the lists equal in length? My country has a balance between _____

_____.

3. What aspects of your country have changed the most in the last 25 years?

_____ have changed the most in the last 25 years.

4. What aspects of your country have not changed in the last 25 years? (Write a complete sentence.)

_____

_____

5. Are there traditions in your country that you do not want to change?

The traditions that I do not want to see change are _____

_____.

Now choose one of the five statements above as the thesis sentence of a composition that you will write.

Supporting
Which thesis sentence have you chosen? This is the main idea of your composition. Look back over your list of traditional and modern aspects. Circle the ideas that support your thesis. Can you think of other supporting ideas to add to your list?

Drafting
Write down your thesis. Create two to three paragraphs that support this idea from your list of circled words and phrases. Summarize what you have said in a concluding sentence.

Revision
Read your composition aloud. Ask yourself these questions:

Is the thesis sentence clear?

Do all of the sentences that follow the thesis support it?

Do the sentences fit together smoothly?

Do I need linking words or phrases to show how the sentences are related?

Does my concluding sentence tie together the other sentences?

Make necessary changes and reread the paragraph for grammar, punctuation, and spelling.

Group Feedback
Get together with the same group that discussed the photograph at the beginning of this chapter. Exchange your composition with a member of the group. Have that person read the composition and then answer the questions in the previous Revision section as you discuss each other's writing.

Draft Again
Using suggestions from the group, write your composition again in the correct form shown on page 8. Give it an interesting title.

LINKING WORDS AND PHRASES THAT SHOW COMPARISON

like	Family life in my country is *like* it was 50 years ago.
likewise	The marriage ceremony is very traditional; *likewise,* the role of women is the same as it was in the past.
in the same way	*in the same way* that religion is respected, the wisdom of elders is valued.
at the same time	Industry is growing *at the same time* as business is developing.
similarly	Many women have college degrees; *similarly,* women work in professions.
once again	Fifty years ago religious rules were followed by most people; *once again* religion has become important.

LINKING WORDS AND PHRASES OF CONTRAST

but	Women have equal education to men in my country, *but* not as many women have jobs.
though, although	*Although* agriculture is important, very few people want to be farmers.
however	Traditional dances are done at weddings; *however,* really good dancers are difficult to find.
nevertheless	Mining is not as important to the economy; *nevertheless,* many students are studying in this field.
yet	The economy continues to be based on oil, *yet* we are developing other industries.
still	My country looks quite modern, *still* it has many traditional customs.
on the other hand	My country is not rich; *on the other hand,* it has a wealth of tradition.

on the contrary	Dating is common in the United States. *On the contrary,* it has never been practiced in my country.
in contrast to	Nigeria, *in contrast to* the United States, is very traditional.
while	My country is developing economically *while* it is losing some of its old customs.

EXERCISES TO POLISH UP YOUR WRITING

Analyze the following student essay to help you to understand how a composition that compares and contrasts can be organized.

Contrasts in Saudi Arabia

My country, Saudi Arabia, is very traditional in areas ruled by religion but is very modern in industry and business. A strong family life and a protected role for women are two traditions that have not changed much during the past 25 years. These traditions come directly from the Islamic religion. For example, families still spend most of their time together. Family members ask each other for advice and, in addition, they respect what older persons have to say. In regard to women, they are very important as teachers of religion to their children. They are protected by the way they must dress in public and by limiting them, more or less, to activities in the home.

In contrast to these traditional parts of my country is the rapid growth Saudi Arabia has made in industry and business. It has become one of the most progressive oil-producing countries in the world. It also is developing other industry and business that will support the country if oil production lessens. In conclusion, Saudi Arabia is a contrast between traditional religious aspects and modern business and industry.

To see how this composition is organized, fill in the blanks in the following outline.

Title: _____

Main Idea: _____

_____

I. Traditional Aspects

    A. _____

        1. Family Time Together

        2. Ask _____

        3. Respect _____

    B. _____

        1. Teachers of Religion

        2. Protected by _____

II. Modern Aspects

    A. _____

    B. _____

    Can you find five words or phrases that help to relate one idea to another in the essay, "Contrasts in Saudi Arabia"?

1. _____   4. _____

2. _____   5. _____

3. _____

As you observed in the essay on Saudi Arabia, linking words and phrases helps to smooth the way for the reader by showing the relationship between ideas.

EXERCISE 6-3 Choosing Linking Words and Phrases

In the following essay, fill in the blank with the correct linking word or phrase from the following list. The use of the word or phrase is given in parentheses:

As you can see, (conclusion)	In contrast to (contrast)
In conclusion, (conclusion)	Yet (contrast)
However, (contrast)	Similarly (comparison)
Though (contrast)	Also (addition)
On the other hand, (contrast)	In addition (addition)

Weather Around the World

Although weather changes each day, the general pattern of temperature and rainfall is fairly similar year after year. This weather pattern is called climate. A country's climate depends on its position on the globe, its height above sea level, and its distance from the sea. _____ local winds have an effect on climate.

It is interesting to look at some extremes in climate in the world. The sunniest place in the world is the Sahara Desert in the Sudan, where there are only about 80 hours a year when it is cloudy during the day. _____ the least sunny place is the South Pole in Antarctica, where in the winter there is no sun at all for nearly 27 weeks. Three countries share the honor of being the hottest: Mali, Upper Volta, and Niger. _____ temperatures in these countries of about 28° C., the coldest places are Antarctica, Greenland and Alaska, with temperatures ranging from −60 to −1° C. _____, Alaska is the country with the worst snow storm in history.

Where is the driest place in the world? The Atacama Desert in Chile had not had any rain for 400 years until it finally rained in 1971. _____, Mt. Wai-ale'ale in Hawaii has only about 6 days a year that it does not rain.

_____ weather in the world provides great extremes, according to location, height, and other factors.

EXERCISE 6-4   **Practice Using Comparison/Contrast Terms**

Study these facts about two students.

Bernardo	*Francisco*
19 years old	21 years old
from Bogota, Colombia	from Bogota, Colombia
has 1 brother	has 3 sisters, 3 brothers
father owns supermarket	father employed by government
plans to study business administration	plans to study accounting
studied English in Colombia for six years	studied English in Colombia for 1 year
likes music and dancing	likes skiing, all sports

Write seven sentences comparing and contrasting the two students. Use the word or phrase in parentheses in the sentence.

EXAMPLE

1. (but) Bernardo is 19 years old, *but* Francisco is 21.

1. (; however,) _____

_____

2. (Both) _____

_____

3. (Although) _____

_____

4. (, but) _____

_____

5. (;) _____

_____

6. (Neither - nor) _____

_____

7. In   contrast   to   Bernardo,   whose   favorite   pastimes   are

_____ and _____ _____,

Francisco likes _____.

THE WEDDING: AN AMERICAN TRADITION

Although the United States does not have a long history, it does have some traditions that are very much a part of its culture. The process through which a couple becomes engaged and eventually married is one of these traditions.

The following description of an actual engagement and wedding will help you to understand this American tradition.

A Traditional American Wedding

Melissa Shoemaker and Mark Hull were married December 21 at 1 P.M. in the United Methodist Church. Melissa was 22 years old and Mark was 24. The happy couple had met three years before and had dated each other all of the time before they married. They had announced their engagement to their parents about three months before the wedding. They sent formal invitations to their friends and relatives more than a month before the wedding. Melissa was very excited about her wedding dress. In the traditional American way, she did not let Mark see the dress before the ceremony. It was a long white gown decorated with pearls. She also wore a lacy white hat and satin shoes and carried a bouquet of roses and carnations as she walked down the aisle of the church on her father's arm. She met her bridegroom, Mark, at the altar, where the bridesmaids and groomsmen were standing.

The minister performed the 45-minute religious ceremony in front of about 125 family members and friends. After the wedding, everyone went to a large reception room in the church to congratulate the bride and groom, to eat wedding cake, to visit with each other, and to listen to music selected by the newly married couple. Before she left on their honeymoon, Melissa threw her bouquet of flowers to the single women who had attended the wedding. The woman who caught the bouquet, according to tradition, would be the next to marry.

Since the bride, who is now called by her husband's last name, is still in college and the groom is starting a new job, they took only two days for their honeymoon in the nearby mountains. Congratulations on your marriage, Melissa and Mark Hull!

Notice how these words were used in the previous story and discuss their usage and meaning with your instructor.

marriage	groom (or bridegroom)
to marry	bridesmaids
wedding	groomsmen
engagement	honeymoon
ceremony	

GETTING IDEAS FOR A COMPOSITION

Questions for Class Discussion

Answer the following questions to help you find out how the traditional American wedding described in the story is different from one in your country.

1. How old, on the average, are young persons in your country when they marry?

2. Where does the ceremony take place? In a church? At home?

3. Is there an engagement? How long are couples engaged?

4. Who chooses the bride? The young man? The family?

5. Do parents have to approve the marriage? What if they do not?

6. Are guests sent formal invitations to the wedding?

7. What does the bride in your country wear? What does the groom wear?

8. Are there groomsmen and bridesmaids? How many? What do they wear?

9. Can the groom see the bride in her dress before the ceremony?

10. What happens during the ceremony?

11. Is there a party after the ceremony? How many people usually come to the party? Do they eat? Do the bride and groom open their gifts at the party?

12. Do young people go away on a honeymoon? If so, where do they go? Where do they live after the honeymoon? With their parents? By themselves?

13. Is the American wedding similar to a wedding in your culture? If not, what are the major differences?

ORGANIZING A COMPARISON-CONTRAST COMPOSITION

If you plan to explain wedding customs in your country by showing similarities and differences with U. S. customs, you will need to organize your composition in one of two ways: block style or alternating style.

Block Style

An outline of a composition organized in **block style** might look like this:

Thesis: Wedding customs in Cyprus are more traditional and formal than those in the United States.

 I. Religion influences customs in Cyprus.
 A. Engagement is announced in church.
 B. Ten to twenty bridesmaids and groomsmen are part of the wedding.
 C. Ceremony remains the same as it was 100 years ago.
 II. Wedding customs vary in the United States.
 A. Engagement is not very important.
 B. Two to four bridesmaids and groomsmen are part of wedding.
 C. Couples can write their own ceremony.

In block style, all the information about customs in Cyprus is mentioned in the first part of the composition. Then all the information about the customs of the United States is discussed in the second paragraph. A third paragraph, which draws some general comparisons and contrasts between the two countries would be added to complete the composition.

Alternating Style

An outline of a composition organized in **alternating style** might look like this:

Thesis: Wedding customs in Cyprus are more traditional and formal than those in the United States. Religion influences customs in Cyprus, but U. S. customs are not always religious.

I. Engagement is different.
   A. Cypriot engagement is announced in church.
   B. U. S. engagement is not very important.
II. Number of bridesmaids, groomsmen varies.
   A. Ten to twenty bridesmaids and groomsmen are part of the Cypriot wedding.
   B. Two to four bridesmaids and groomsmen are part of the U. S. wedding.
III. Ceremony reflects customs.
   A. Cypriot ceremony is the same as it was 100 years ago.
   B. U. S. couples can write their own ceremony.

Notice that the information in this outline is the same as that in the previous outline, but it is organized in alternating fashion, first a discussion of one point in Cyprus and then a discussion of the same custom in the United States, and so on.

The choice of which of these two methods of organization should be used is up to you. Often the details and facts you use to support your thesis sentence will suggest that one method or the other is better. In any case, keep the order within the subdivisions the same; it will help your readers follow the ideas.

ANALYZING A COMPARISON-CONTRAST COMPOSITION

A student from Thailand, who was trying to decide which of two men to marry, wrote the following comparison-contrast composition.

Krittaka Suwannacheep
Intermediate Writing
Professor Moriarity
June 19, 1988

Two Men in My Life

Love is a strong feeling of fondness for another person, especially between members of a family or between people of the opposite sex. There are two men in my life whom I will love forever, Wiwat and Wisuth. I will always remember both their different characteristics and their similar traits.

For example, they are quite similar in physical appearance. Both men have black hair, black eyes, and yellow skin. Wiwat is 29 years old and is of medium build. On the other hand, Wisuth is 34 years old, is fairly tall, and a little fat. In their mental traits, however, there are differences, such as their education. Wiwat earned his bachelor's degree from Bangkok University, majoring in finance. He enjoys mathematics and problem solving. In contrast, Wisuth finished medical school in Bangkok and studied his specialty in the U. S. One, therefore, is a merchant and the other is a doctor. Wiwat plans to be a good merchant and to communicate well with foreign companies. He sells furniture, mattresses, pillows, and other household goods. Wisuth's goal is different. He wants to become a well-known doctor, specializing in heart disease and gerontology. At one time, he worked in a first-class hospital in Thailand. Now, he is practicing in Chicago at St. Francis Hospital.

Furthermore, there are similarities in their personality traits. Each has a very polite manner and is very kind. Nonetheless, differences are obvious. Wiwat looks sincere, mature, calm, sometimes serious and strict, whereas Wisuth speaks softly, is neat and clean—an understanding person but a bit secretive. In addition, they are alike in being diligent, ambitious, and highly self-confident. In spite of this, they have different habits. Wiwat likes Chinese food, enjoys listening to music, loves to jog in the park every Sunday morning, and dislikes shopping. Wisuth enjoys reading medical books and playing tennis. He doesn't like snacking and waiting in crowded restaurants.

In conclusion, when I compare and contrast the two men, it is very difficult for me to choose between them. Consequently, I must take more time to consider my decision as to whom I will marry.

QUESTIONS FOR CLASS DISCUSSION

Answer the following questions about the previous essay.

1. Which method of organization does this writer use? Block or alternating?

2. What is the writer's thesis?

3. What differences and similarities does she discuss? (The first one is physical appearance.)

4. There are at least 12 linking words and phrases in this composition. What are they?

5. If the writer had used block style (discussing one person completely and then the other), would she have used as many linking words? Why or why not?

6. How does she conclude the composition? Was this conclusion a surprise? Would you like the composition to begin with this concluding idea? Why or why not?

EXERCISE 6-5 Writing a Comparison-Contrast Composition

Using the material discussed in this section of the chapter, write a composition of two to three paragraphs. Discuss the similarities and differences between marriage in your country and in the United States. Follow the writing process as shown in the beginning of this chapter. Also prepare a final outline of the composition. Use the formal outline form similar to that on page 199.

EXERCISE 6-6 *Sentence Combining for Comparison-Contrast*

The following short sentences compare and contrast. Choose the best word to combine the short sentences into longer, related ones.

EXAMPLE
Many Americans are getting married in their thirties.
Many Americans are having only one or two children.

Combined: Many Americans are getting married in their thirties *and* having only one or two children.

1. American parents do not arrange marriages.
American parents like to give their OK to the marriage.

_____

2. Weddings cost thousands of dollars in Kuwait.
Weddings cost thousands of dollars in Saudi Arabia.
The reason they cost so much money is that hundreds of people come to the party.

_____

3. In the United States, the groom pays for the flowers for the bride and
   her bridesmaids.
   The groom pays the minister.
   The groom pays for rental of suits for himself and the groomsmen.

   _____

4. The bride's parents usually pay for the wedding dress.
   The bride's parents pay for the flowers for the church.
   The bride's parents also pay for the wedding party and for the photo-
   graphs.

   _____

5. In the United States, the bride and groom kiss at the end of the wedding.
   In Japan, the bride and groom drink rice wine from the same cup at the
   end of the wedding.

   _____

6. At their engagement, the man gives the woman a diamond ring.
   During the ceremony, the man and woman also give each other gold
   rings.

   _____

7. Traditional dances always are part of Greek weddings.
   Modern dances sometimes are part of wedding parties in the United
   States.

   _____

8. Money is given as a gift to young couples in many countries.
   Gifts for the new home usually are given to young people in the United
   States.

   _____

9. Trips to other cities are common honeymoons in the United States.
   Trips to other cities are common honeymoons in Korea and Japan.

   _____

10. Weddings are happy events in all countries.
    The mothers of the bride and groom usually cry.

   _____

WRITING INTRODUCTIONS

The first paragraph of a comoposition must be an *attention-getter*. In other words, the beginning of your composition must be interesting enough for your reader to say, "I wonder what will come next?" or "That's an interesting idea. I wonder how the writer will support it."

Let's look at a few of the ways to get your readers' attention in the first paragraph. Each of the examples that follow is based on the same topic: "A Tradition I Do Not Want to Change." The thesis sentence in each introductory paragraph is in italics.

Begin With a Quotation From a Book, a Magazine, or Use a Proverb.

"The ways of your ancestors are good. They cannot be blown away by the winds because their roots reach deep into the soil." This statement by Otek P'Bitek expresses my strong feeling about the tradition of arranged marriage in my country. *Because arranged marriages are happy and lasting, this is a tradition I do not want to see "blown away by the winds" of change.*

Begin With a General Statement Related to Your Topic.

Traditions give security and continuity to a culture. A tradition is like an anchor that holds a ship in one place in spite of storms at sea. *A strong family life is a tradition in my culture and one that I hope will continue forever.*

Begin With the Definition of a Word That is Important to Your Topic.

Tradition is defined as the passing down of elements of a culture from generation to generation. In my culture, telling the stories of the prophets is a tradition that is passed from old to young. *This tradition of storytelling is an important element of the culture that I hope will never change.*

Begin With a Question Related To The Topic.

Just how important is tradition in Korean culture? My answer to this question is "Very important!" Tradition is what keeps the people of my country unified and cohesive. One of the most important traditions is respect for the eldest member of the family or community. *This traditional respect is an element of my culture that will not change with the influence of modern times.*

Begin With a Related Fact.

Eighty percent of all Greek Cypriot young people continue their educations with degrees from universities and colleges. *This tradition of respect for higher educa-*

tion is an important aspect of Greek culture that will continue, I hope, for many thousands of years.

REVISION EXERCISES

REVISION EXERCISE 1   Writing Introductions

Using the thesis sentence that you wrote for Exercise 6-6, a comparison of marriage in your country and the United States, write three different kinds of introductory paragraphs. Choose three of the five types discussed previously. Write a few sentences of introduction and end the paragraph with the thesis statement that you used in Exercise 6-6. Underline the thesis.

EXAMPLE
    Quotation Beginning
        When Americans speak of getting married, they often say, "We're going to tie the knot." It seems to me, however, that the knot of an American marriage is very loosely tied, whereas the marriage knot in Malaysian culture is tight and difficult to untie.

REVISION EXERCISE 2   Using a Consistent Block or Alternating Style

A good writer is consistent in the style he chooses. Earlier in this chapter, you studied two styles of organizing a comparison-contrast composition: block or alternating style. The composition that follows has some inconsistencies in style. Read the composition and answer the questions that follow.

Los Angeles and San Francisco

Two of the greatest cities in the United States—Los Angeles and San Francisco—are in California. Even though both cities are in the same state, they are very different in location, population, and types of businesses.

Los Angeles and its suburbs spread across the southern part of California. This city has a scenic location with a warm, pleasant southern climate and an outdoor way of life. Beaches line the Pacific Ocean to the west and south of the city, and tall mountains rise to the northeast. In regard to population, Los Angeles is the second largest city in the United States with a population of about 3 million people. More than half the people of Los Angeles and its surrounding county moved there from other parts of the United States or from other countries.

Whereas Los Angeles includes many immigrants from nearby Mexico, San Francisco has been called "the most Asian" city on the mainland of the United States because of its large population of Chinese, Japanese, Philippine, Korean, and Vietnamese people. San Francisco also is located in a different area of California. It sits on high hillsides above San Francisco Bay in the central part of California. Some of the more than 40 hills rise as high as 376 feet (115 meters). Sparkling blue water almost surrounds San Francisco and makes it a beautiful attraction for tourists.

In terms of business, Los Angeles is a business, financial, and trade center of the Western United States. It leads the nation in production of aircraft and equipment for space exploration. In addition, the city's motion picture and television industry is world famous. San Francisco, on the other hand, is a leader in food processing and machinery building.

In summary, these two interesting California cities have some major differences in location and appearance, population size and variety of nationalities, and types of business.

1. What three points in the main idea are set up for discussion in the composition?

2. Which of the two cities is discussed in the second paragraph? Which points about this city are discussed here? After reading the second paragraph, what style of organization do you believe the writer is going to use—block or alternating?

3. Which city is discussed in the third paragraph? What points (location, population, business) are discussed in this paragraph? What is inconsistent about this paragraph?

4. Which city is discussed in the fourth paragraph? What points (location, population, business) are discussed here? What is inconsistent in this paragraph? What style of organization (block or alternating) is used in paragraph four?

5. How would you revise the composition to correct the inconsistencies in organization?

6. Rewrite the third and fourth paragraphs so that the composition consistently follows the block style of organization.

FOR WRITERS WHO HAVE MORE TO SAY

Journal Assignment

Write about the greatest difference you have noticed between your culture and American culture. How have you adjusted to this difference?

Are there contrasting cultures within your country? Write about the similarities and differences between these cultures.

Class Assignment

Interview a student from another culture to find out the differences and similarities in one of the following customs:

Eating habits and favorite foods

Traditional dress

Important holidays

Treatment of older people

Write a two to three paragraph composition based on the interview.

CHAPTER SUMMARY

Listing is a useful method of getting ideas for a comparison-contrast composition.

Block or alternating style are the two ways of organizing a writing assignment that compares and contrasts.

In block style, all the information about one group is discussed first. Then all the information about the group being compared is discussed next.

In alternating style, one point about the first group is discussed, then the same point about the second group, and so on.

Linking words and phrases are particularly important in comparison-contrast writing because they draw the readers' attention to similarities and differences.

Introductions are important as attention-getters in all kinds of writing. The five kinds of introductions include:

quotation

general statement

definition

question

related fact.

CHAPTER 7

A Mouse and a Second Language

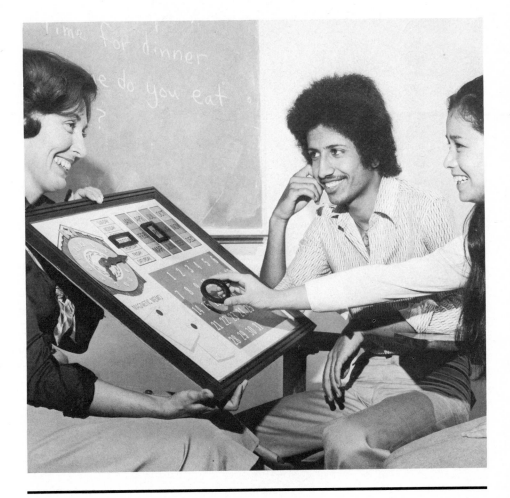

See how it pays to know a second language?

—Mother Mouse

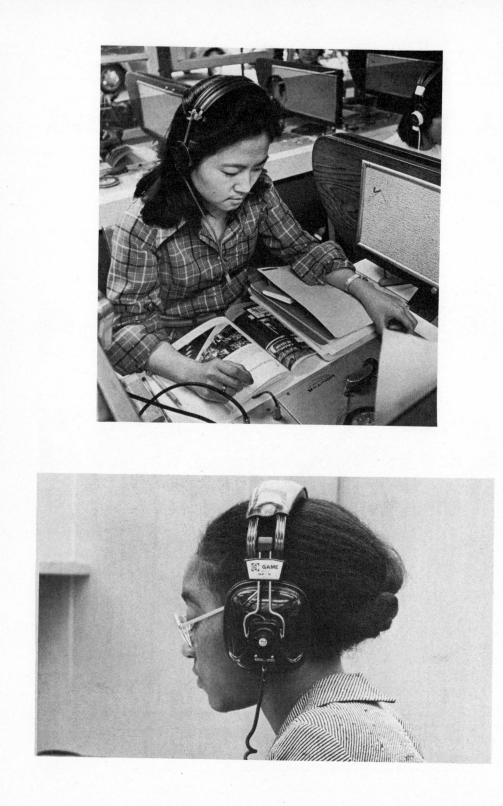

One day a mother mouse was taking her mouse children for a walk. As the little family turned the corner of a building, they found themselves facing a large, hungry cat with twitching whiskers. The mother mouse was a very quick thinker. She made herself as tall as she could, drew in a huge breath of air, and shouted, "Woof, woof!" in the loudest possible voice. The surprised cat turned and ran down the street as fast as possible. As the cat disappeared, the mother mouse turned to her children and said, with great wisdom, "See how it pays to know a second language!"

As a student of English, you already know how important it is to learn a second language. Knowing a second language might possibly save your life in a dangerous situation, as in the story of the mouse family. But, more probably, your knowledge of English will be the key that opens the door to a university education, a good job, and knowledge of another culture.

JOURNAL ASSIGNMENT

What doors do you hope English will open for you in the future? Why did you choose to study English rather than another language?

USING THE WRITING PROCESS TO ANALYZE A PROCESS

Why you are learning a second language is probably very clear to you, but have you ever thought about how you are learning this language? What steps are you following? What process are you going through?

A process is a series of actions leading to a planned result.

In other words, the process of learning English consists of several steps or stages that lead to a full command of the language. When you write about a process, you can do one of two things: 1) instruct or direct your readers on how to follow the process or 2) explain or analyze the process to tell how it is done, how it happens, or how it works.

Let's use learning a second language as an example: If you are going to write about this topic, you probably will want to explain or analyze how a learner acquires a second language.

GETTING IDEAS: SMALL GROUP EXERCISE

To gather the most ideas about language learning, it will be helpful to share the experience of other students. Divide into groups of three to four students. Appoint one group member to record your ideas on a sheet of paper. Discuss this question and list ideas:

What are the actions one goes through to learn a second language?

Spend only about 5-10 minutes in discussing and making your list of ideas. Then, as a group, study the list and try to reach agreement on the order in which the actions take place. Number the actions. Do they always happen in the same order? Are any of them ever repeated during the process of learning a language?

Each group may wish to share its list to see if there are other ideas to add. Is the list complete?

FOCUSING

As you think about the class list of steps in learning a second language, what do you notice? Are there many steps? Are they simple? Are they complex? Your thesis for a process composition can be as simple as "There are six major steps in learning a second language." However, it is more interesting to have a stronger and more specific thesis; in other words, to say something *about* the process.

Write two possible thesis statements here:

1. _____

   _____

2. _____

   _____

What is a good thesis statement?
1. A good thesis statement says something specific about a topic; it is not too general.

2. A good thesis expresses the writer's attitude toward a topic.

3. A good thesis is expressed in a complete, clear sentence.

Review your two thesis statements with these three points in mind. Is each of your statements a good thesis?

Examples of Weak and Revised Thesis Statements
Study these examples of weak thesis statements (on the left) and notice how they have been revised (on the right) into stronger statements. The thesis statements were written by intermediate students for a composition on "Why They Chose to Study in the United States."

Weak Theses	Revised Theses
I like the United States, so I came here to study.	I have always admired the educational system in the United States, so I came here to study.
I came to this country with my brother and two cousins.	I chose to study in the United States because I wanted to live with people from my own family—my brother and two cousins.
Freedom is important to me, so I came to the United States to study.	Political freedom is important to me, so I came to the United States to study.
Because my government gave me a scholarship to study engineering.	I am studying in the United States because my government gave me a scholarship to study engineering here.
Studying in the United States is nice.	I have chosen to study in the United States because the standard of living is comfortable and the people are friendly.
Culture is important in everyone's life.	Learning about another culture is an important experience not everyone is able to have; that's why I have chosen to study in the United States.

Now that you have studied a list of weak and strong thesis statements, you should be ready to recognize good thesis sentences.

EXERCISE 7-1   **Judging thesis statements**

Study the following thesis statements for a composition on the process of learning a second language. Check (√) each good thesis statement. Next to each sentence that you do not think is a good thesis, write the number of the quality that would make it better: 1) A good thesis says something specific about a topic. 2) A good thesis expresses the writer's attitude toward a topic. 3) A good thesis is expressed in a complete, clear sentence.

EXAMPLE

___*1*___ Languages are fun.

_____ 1. Learning a second language is a very complex process.
_____ 2. Language learning is a big problem.
_____ 3. The difficulties of learning English.
_____ 4. Learning a second language is more difficult than learning your first language.
_____ 5. There are three major stages in learning a second language.

_____ 6. Climbing the mountain of language learning.
_____ 7. Learning a second language is very much like climbing a mountain; in order to succeed, you must keep your mind on your goal.
_____ 8. Learning a second language is a good idea.
_____ 9. Is learning a language difficult?
_____ 10. I love languages because they open the door to many cultures.

SUPPORTING YOUR FOCUS

Choose a thesis statement from the two possibilities on page 140 or from the good theses in Exercise 7-1. This sentence will be the focus for a composition of several paragraphs about the process of learning a second language. Write your thesis statement here.

_____

_____

REVISING THESIS STATEMENTS

The first thesis statement you write may have all the qualities of a good thesis, but that does not mean that it cannot be changed as you write your composition. In fact, the formation of a thesis is a process of changes and adjustments to fit the growing composition.

For example, a student wrote this beginning thesis statement after she had listed her ideas about adjustment to a new culture:

My adjustment to American culture involved four distinct steps leading to my goal of acting like an American.

After she had written a rough draft, she discovered something important: Her goal was not to act like an American but to feel comfortable in the new culture. She rewrote the thesis to read:

My adjustment to American culture involved four distinct steps that finally led to my goal of feeling comfortable here.

After she had revised further, she thought about the word *steps:* it did not seem to fit her description of the process of adjustment. She changed this word to *stages.*

As you can see, forming a thesis continues until the composition is finished.

Remember that the thesis you have chosen is the idea that controls and ties together all the separate elements in your composition. If you have said that learning a language is a difficult process, then it will be necessary to show how difficult the steps are. Or, if you have said that learning a second language is more difficult than learning a first language, you will have to prove to your readers that it is, indeed, more difficult.

As you plan your composition, check over this list of hints:

HINTS FOR WRITING A PROCESS COMPOSITION

1. **Discuss the steps chronologically.** A process composition describes a series of steps leading to an expected end; it is important to discuss the steps in the order in which they happen. Move away from this order only when you need to explain some unfamiliar term or give some word of advice.

2. **Be certain that the process is complete.** Make certain you have included all the steps in the process. If one step is left out, the reader will not be able to complete the process.

3. **Keep your audience in mind.** When you are planning a process composition, the first question is "What does my reader know about the topic?" The answer to this question will help you to decide how much explanation and detail is needed in the composition. Since your audience is students involved in learning a second language and a teacher of this subject, you will need to give them some new and interesting ideas about language learning.

4. **Explain the purpose of a step.** A process composition is more than just a list of steps. If the reason behind a step in the process of language learning is not clear, you will need to explain the reason for the action.

5. **Warn your readers of difficulties in the process.** When planning how to support your focus, try to think of the problems you may have experienced and warn your readers of these.

EXERCISE 7-2 Revising Thesis Statements

Change these preliminary thesis statements to fit the support that developed as the writer composed.

1. My country has developed more since its independence than it did in the previous 300 years.
(The student focused on only two aspects of development: education and industry.)

---

2. I prefer to live in the city because it provides better educational opportunities than the small town.
   (As the student wrote, he decided to include the sports activities and entertainment possibilities of the big city.)

   _____

   _____

3. Television is a waste of time for children and leads to behavior problems.
   (The student read several articles that proved through research that educational programs can greatly improve a child's vocabulary and understanding of the world.)

   _____

   _____

4. The major turning point of my life was traveling to the United States.
   (As the composition developed, the writer emphasized independence from his parents which led him to become self-sufficient and stronger rather than the general idea of traveling to the United States.)

   _____

   _____

5. I learned an important lesson from my first automobile accident: never drive in a foreign country.
   (The writer decided that the real lesson was that he should know the local rules before driving.)

   _____

   _____

EXERCISE 7-3   Planning the Process Composition

Using the hints at the right, fill in the blanks with phrases that indicate the order of ideas in your composition.

    I. Introduction

                                                     Introduce the topic and your purpose for writing about it.

_____   State your thesis.

_____

_____

_____

II. Supporting Paragraphs

Begin describing the steps. Smaller steps may be combined into three or four major steps. Each of the major steps may take a separate paragraph.

_____

_____

_____

_____

_____

_____

_____

_____

III. Conclusion

The conclusion often discusses the results of the process being described. You may also discuss the benefits of the process.

_____

_____

_____

_____

DRAFTING, REVISING AND DRAFTING AGAIN

EXERCISE 7-4 Completing the Process Composition

Using the plan in Exercise 7-3, write the rough draft of your process essay. When you have finished, read it aloud to check for these points:

Do I have a clear thesis?

Does everything in the composition support this thesis?

Have I included all of the important steps?

Have I explained the purpose of a step when necessary?

Have I kept my audience in mind?

Have I concluded the composition in an interesting way?

Also refer to your editing checklist, page 243, to make certain you have avoided your most common mistakes. Make necessary revisions; then correct for errors in spelling, grammar, and punctuation. Rewrite in correct form.

If you would like further suggestions for revision, share the draft with a classmate. Ask him the questions above, plus this one: Could you follow the steps in the composition and actually complete the process I have written about? Use your classmate's suggestions. Draft again if necessary and present the composition to your instructor for further suggestions.

EXAMPLE OF A PROCESS ANALYSIS ESSAY

The Decision-Making Process

Decision making is one of the most important tasks of a business manager. Decision making may be defined as the process of choosing a course of action to solve a particular problem. The ideal decision-making process includes six major steps.

The first step is to define the problem. This difficult action involves careful analysis of a situation in order to state the problem and find out what has caused it. For example, a restaurant may be giving slow, inadequate service to its customers (the problem) because the dining-room manager has not scheduled enough waiters during the busiest hours (the cause). Defining the problem is absolutely necessary to a good, clear-cut decision.

The second step, defining the expectation, involves stating the result that is expected once the problem has been solved. The expected result after solving the problem of poor service in the restaurant would be to raise the quality of service to the diners.

After defining the expectation, data are gathered about the problem. In the case of the restaurant, the data might be simply the employee schedule and the chart that shows the relationship between numbers of customers and time of day. In a more complicated problem, the data might include observations, surveys, or published research. Many businesses use computers to process, summarize, and report data. A manager must have sufficient data before going to the next step.

In this step, the decision maker develops possible solutions to the problem. In the restaurant example, one solution might be to replace the dining-room manager. Another solution might be to give the present manager of the dining room the necessary information about busy times of day and available waiters and suggest to him better ways to make efficient assignments.

In the fifth step, the decision maker looks at the possible solutions in terms of the expected result to increase the quality of service to diners and any limitations, such as time and money. Solution one, above, replacing the dining-room manager, does not make certain that there will be better service and it would involve training a new manager. Solution 2, giving all possible information and some suggestions for scheduling, would take time but should bring about the better service needed.

Finally, the decision maker compares the solutions and chooses the one that may provide the results needed. In the case of the dining-room manager, the decision maker decides to give information to the manager and suggest ways of scheduling the available waiters in order to improve customer service.

The decision-making process is followed by putting into action the chosen solution and evaluating it to see if it is successful. This six-step process is valuable not just for business managers but also for anyone facing a problem.

QUESTIONS FOR CLASS DISCUSSION

1. What is the thesis statement of the previous essay? (Remember that a good thesis states the writer's attitude toward his subject.)

2. What is the purpose of the second sentence in the essay? Why is this sentence necessary for you as an audience?

3. Look at the way in which paragraphs are divided. What is the writer's plan in dividing his essay in this way?

4. The writer does not just *list* the steps. How does he further develop each step?

5. Are the steps clearly explained? Is the process complete?

6. What transition words mark the sequence of steps? Underline these in the essay.

7. How does the writer conclude the essay?

8. Underline the verbs in each sentence. What verb tenses are used?

EXERCISE 7-5   **Outlining a Process Composition**

Outline the essay "The Decision-Making Process." Use these major headings: I. Introduction, II. Steps in the Procedure, and III. Conclusion. Check page 199 for proper outline form.

POLISHING YOUR WRITING

In writing compositions that analyze or describe a process, you will need to draw your readers' attention to the order of steps. Time words will achieve this purpose.

Word and Phrases that Show Order in Time

first, second, etc.	*First,* you must have the correct change. You *first* must have the correct change.
next	*Next,* you lift the telephone receiver and listen for the dial tone. You *next* lift the telphone receiver and listen for the dial tone.
in the next place	*In the next place,* it is necessary to deposit 20 cents in the slot.
subsequently	*Subsequently,* it is essential to correctly dial the number. It is necessary *subsequently* to correctly dial the number.
then	*Then* listen for a busy signal. You *then* should listen for a busy signal.
after that	*After that,* you should feel proud of using an American pay phone. You should feel proud of using an American pay phone *after that.*
afterward	*Afterward,* try placing an international call on a private line.
simultaneously	My friend can talk on the telephone and do her homework *simultaneously.* *Simultaneously,* my friend can talk on the telephone and do her homework.
finally	*Finally,* you may wish to try placing an international call on a private line.
later	*Later,* you may wish to place an international call on a private line.
lastly	*Lastly,* you may wish to place an international call on a private line.
prior to	*Prior to* placing the call, check with the operator to see if you can dial country-to-country. *Prior to* the call, check with the operator to see if you can dial country-to-country. Check with the operator *prior to* the call.
after	*After* completing the call, you can check on the charges if you have made arrangements prior to the call.

	After you complete the call, you can check on the charges if you have made arrangements prior to the call.
	You can check on the charges *after* you complete the call.
while	*While* talking long distance, you may wish to check the time occasionally.
	While you talk long distance, you may wish to check the time occasionally.
	You may wish to check the time occasionally *while* you talk long distance.
before	*Before* making too many international calls, know the times and days that are least expensive.
	Before you make too many international calls, know the times and days that are least expensive.
	Know the times and days that are least expensive *before* you make too many international calls.

Note: As important as time words are, they should not be used at the beginning of every sentence. Read your composition to see if the meaning would still be clear if you left out some of the time words or try placing some of the time words *within* the sentence rather than at the beginning. (See examples above.)

The exercise that follows is an example of a process composition that is clear in time order without the use of too many time words.

EXERCISE 7-6   Using Words of Time Order

Fill in the blanks in this composition with appropriate time words.

How To Make Friends in the Cafeteria

Every international student should have American friends to help him practice his English and to teach him about American culture. However, this is easier said than done. Because of limited English and shyness in a new culture, the international student has great difficulty getting acquainted with Americans. However, it is possible to make friends if you follow these six steps.

_____ go to the college or university cafeteria at the busiest time of day and order your lunch plus an extra package of French fries or a delicious-looking dessert. _____ look around for a table occupied by only one person. Check to see that this person is not intent on studying for an exam. _____ approach the person and introduce yourself. You might say, "Hi, I'm Silvia. Would you mind if I shared your table?"

If you're invited to sit down, _____ the hardest part is over. _____ politely eating your lunch, ask the American questions about his or her major, classes, and so on. Beware of becoming too personal at this first meeting. You might even offer that extra serving of fries or the dessert. _____ you've finished eating, you should show your interest in meeting your acquaintance again. "Maybe we can have lunch again sometime this week," is a good way to show your interest in getting better acquainted.

In summary, getting acquainted with an American in the cafeteria isn't as difficult as you may have imagined. It just takes a little bravery, a lunch, and a few English phrases.

EXERCISE 7-7   Writing Statements of Time Order

The following sentences use time order words, such as *prior to* and *while.* Fill in the blanks with words or phrases that fit the order of actions.

EXAMPLE

While *listening to the lecture,* take notes very carefully.

1. Prior to _____, you should gather all the ingredients for the cake.

2. To begin with, you must _____ in order to score 550 on the TOEFL.

3. While _____, prepare the rice.

4. Before _____, turn the key in the ignition.

5. Apply for your visa; then _____

_____.

6. Put two dimes in the pay telephone; after that _____

_____

7. To prepare a fried egg, first _____

_____. Then _____.

8. After _____, the soccer captain flips a coin into

the air.

9. While _____, I also like to study.

10. Listening skill comes first; subsequently _____.

11. After _____, put the car in first gear by depress-

ing the clutch pedal and moving the gear shift to first position. Keep your

foot on the clutch pedal while simultaneously _____

_____. In this way, the car should move forward

smoothly.

12. Paint the ceiling of the room first; later, _____

_____.

Combining Sentences for Coherence

In Chapter 3, page 60, you learned how to combine sentences using adverbial clauses. Since process essays also are organized chronologically, it is possible to combine short sentences to show the relationship in time between one event and another. Most of the sentences in the previous exercise are examples of this type of combination. Here is another example:

EXAMPLE
   After I had listened to the sounds of English, I was ready to try pronouncing some
      of the words.

This example includes an adverbial clause of time

   After I had listened to the sounds of English.

and an independent clause

   I was ready to try pronouncing some of the words.

   Often, in process compositions, you will talk to your reader by using the
pronoun *you* in the first clause and a command in the second clause.

EXAMPLE
   First, you will need to peel the potatoes; then place them in boiling water.

As you will notice, the *you* has been dropped from "then place them in boiling
water."

EXERCISE 7-8   **Combining Sentences with Adverbial Clauses**

Combine the two short sentences into one sentence that shows the correct
time relationship. Use transition words such as *before, after, when, as,* and
while.

EXAMPLE
   You decide on your major.
   You do research on universities that offer it.
   Combined: After you decide on your major, do research on universities
      that offer it.

1. You go to the reference section of the library.
   You locate a copy of *The College Handbook.*

   _____

   _____

2. You look in the index under your major field.
   You will find a list of all colleges and universities that offer your major.

   _____

   _____

3. You study the entrance requirements of these universities.
   You choose the areas of the United States you would like to live in.

   _____

   _____

4. You choose five universities for which you qualify.
   You write to each of these for information about admission.

   _____

   _____

5. You wait for a reply.
   You do further research on the advantages and disadvantages of studying at these universities.

   _____

   _____

6. You receive information from your top choices.
   You make application to at least three of the five.

   _____

   _____

7. You write a short essay for admission.
   You revise and edit it carefully.

   _____

   _____

Shortening Adverbial Clauses to Participial Phrases

In Exercise 7-8, you combined sentences with adverbial clauses of time. To add variety in sentence structure to your writing, these same clauses can be shortened, or reduced, to participial phrases.

EXAMPLE

> You go to the reference section of the library.
> You locate a copy of *The College Handbook*.

Adverbial clause: After you go to the reference section of the library, locate a copy of *The College Handbook*.

Participial phrase: After going to the reference section of the library, locate a copy of *The College Handbook*.

EXERCISE 7-9   Use of Participial Phrases

In sentences 2-7 of Exercise 7-8, shorten the adverbial clause to a participial phrase. Write the new sentences on a separate sheet of paper. Number 1 has been done for you in the example above.

INSTRUCTING READERS HOW TO FOLLOW A PROCESS

In the first part of this chapter, you wrote a composition that analyzed a process. Your purpose in this essay was to show how one learns a language. This is one type of process essay. The other type explains **how to do something.** The purpose of this type of essay is to make the steps in a process so clear that the reader can follow them and get the expected results. Although the purposes of these two types of process essays are different, the patterns of development and organization are the same.

An example of a how-to-do-it process essay will show you the differences that come from purpose.

Example of a Process Composition that Instructs

George Keriotis
Intermediate Writing
Professor Freemont
August 8, 1988

How to Make a Greek Feta Cheese Salad

Feta cheese is to Greek cooking what parmesan is to the Italians, cheddar to the British, Brie to the French, and plain old processed American is to the Americans. The pure white, crumbly cheese with a salty flavor is used for everything from appetizer to accent to binder, giving Greek dishes a character all their own. One of the easiest ways to introduce the use of feta cheese is in a Greek Feta Cheese Salad. Even the most inexperienced cook can make this delightful salad.

Basic steps in the process of making this salad are preparation of the ingredients, mixing of the dressing, and tossing of the salad. Ingredients needed for the salad include:

12 ounces feta cheese

6 tablespoons olive oil

3 tablespoons wine vinegar

½ teaspoon coarsely ground black pepper

2 stalks celery

½ head Belgian endive

¼ teaspoon salt

1 ounce shelled pecans

After gathering the ingredients, you should dice the cheese and place it in a bowl. In another small bowl, beat together ¼ cup (4 tablespoons) oil, one tablespoon vinegar and the pepper. Sprinkle dressing over the cheese. Then cover this mixture and let stand at room temperature 40 minutes. Next, slice the celery into about ⅛ inch slices and cut the endive in a salad bowl. Then mix together the remaining oil and vinegar; add salt. To finish up the salad, pour dressing over it. Carefully add cheese and top with the pecans.

These simple steps of preparation of ingredients, mixing of dressing, and tossing of the salad lead to a finished product that pleases all tastes. The completed salad has a delightful mixture of colors and flavors and is the beginning to a complete Greek menu.

QUESTIONS FOR CLASS DISCUSSION

1. How does the writer introduce his topic? Is this a good beginning? Why or why not?

2. Definitions usually are part of process compositions. What does the writer use in the first paragraph that is like a definition?

3. What sentence (or sentences) includes the thesis statement for this composition? Underline the thesis.

4. What is the main idea of the second paragraph? Where else in the composition do you see this main idea repeated?

5. Are the ingredients specific enough? Would you be able to prepare the ingredients from this list? Is there other information you might need to know as an international student audience?

6. What does the third paragraph include? Can you find a sentence that uses a participial phrase? Underline it. Underline all verbs in the imperative mood (command form). Underline all transition words of time.

7. How does the writer conclude the composition?

8. Would you consider this a good process composition? Why? Why not?

Qualities of a good process composition

1. **A clear, limiting title**   Make your title say exactly what you are giving instructions for doing or making. For example, "Instructions for Changing a Flat Automobile Tire" is a better title than "How to Take Care of Your Car in an Emergency."

2. **Informed content**   Know what you are writing about.

3. **Logically ordered steps**   Good instructions not only divide the process into steps; they also guide readers through the steps in order, so mistakes will not happen.

4. **Correct level of technicality**   Unless you know that readers have a technical background, write for general readers, and do two things. First, give them enough background to understand why they should follow the instructions. Second, give explanations that are detailed enough that your readers can easily understand.

5. **Details**   Provide enough details for readers to understand and repeat the process successfully.

6. **Visual aids**   Whenever you need to, use a diagram or picture to illustrate a point.

7. **Active voice and imperative mood**   The active voice (A nail pierced the tire) speaks more directly than the passive (The tire was pierced by a nail). Likewise, the imperative mood (Open the door) gives more authority to your instructions than the indicative mood (You open the door).

8. **Linking words to mark time and order**   Linking words are like bridges between related ideas. Examples from the previous composition: *after, then, next, to finish up.*

WRITING A PROCESS COMPOSITION THAT INSTRUCTS

Choose one of these two topics: "Heading, an Important Skill for a Soccer Player," or "How to Play Bingo." Then, using the illustrations and information that accompany your chosen topic, write a composition of three to five paragraphs that includes the following parts:

Title

I. Introduction
   A. Purpose of learning the skill
   B. Definition or brief description of the procedure
   C. Your attitude toward the process (thesis)
   D. Materials, equipment, special conditions for using the process
   E. List of major steps
II. Steps in the Procedure
   A. First major step
   B. Second major step
   C. Third major step
III. Conclusion
   A. Summary of major steps
   B. Description of results

Heading, a method of moving the soccer ball down the field

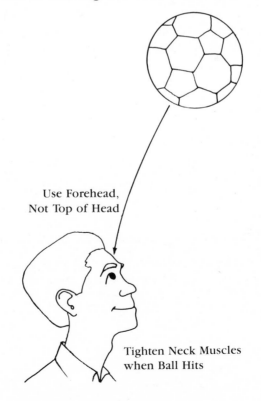

Use Forehead, Not Top of Head

Tighten Neck Muscles when Ball Hits

Get in position to meet the ball at the right moment. Reaching the ball too soon or too late will ruin your effort.

The power of heading comes from the movement of your trunk from your hips. Neck muscles, shoulder muscles—all the power of your upper body—must come into play.

How to Play Bingo

Object of the game: To cover a row of numbers on a card in any of three directions: horizontally, vertically, or diagonally.

WRITING TITLES

As you have seen in this and previous chapters, a good title is a great help to the reader. Not only does it tell the reader something about the topic, but a good title is the writer's first chance to attract the reader's interest and encourage him to read further. You will therefore want to study the following information on the Qualities of a Good Title.

B I N G O

1 TO 15	16 TO 30	31 TO 45	46 TO 60	61 TO 75
13	27	38	47	64
4	20	40	50	70
11	28	★	48	66
15	19	43	54	68
7	29	31	55	65

Bingo Card

BINGO DISPENSER

Bingo Dispenser

O-63   B-6   I-19   N-33   G-54

Plastic Call Numbers and Markers

Qualities of a Good Title

1. **Short**   They should take up less than one line on the page.

2. **Specific**   They should say what the composition is about. It is best to write the title after you have finished your first draft or, at least, after you have written your thesis statement. That way you will know more specifically what your composition is about.

3. **Properly capitalized**   The first word and all major words of the title should be capitalized. Articles, prepositions, and conjunctions, unless they are the first word, should not be capitalized.

Examples of Titles

Weak or Incorrect	*Rewritten*
The Difficulties of Performing the Process of developing color film	The Process of Developing Color Film
How to prepare Indian curry	How to Prepare Indian Curry
Writing a Letter	How to Write a Complaint Letter

My first day in California was disappointing	A Disappointing Day in California
Six Steps in the Process of Learning English as a Second Language	Learning English: a Six-Step Process
A Day In The Countryside	A Day in the Countryside
My Reasons for Studying	My Reasons for Studying Chemistry
The person I most admire	My Brother: The Person I Most Admire

The Revision Exercise that follows should give you practice in recognizing good titles.

REVISION EXERCISES

REVISION EXERCISE   Judging Titles

Keeping in mind the qualities of a good title, judge the following titles. Next to each well written and properly capitalized title, place a check (√) mark. Titles that are not well written should be rewritten in the space beneath.

EXAMPLE

_____ Driver's license

How to Get a Driver's License in the United States

_____ 1. How to Head a Soccer Ball

_____ 2. The Card Catalog

_____ 3. The Process of Making Japanese Sushi

_____ 4. The Seven Easy Steps a Beginner Needs to Follow to Learn to Play the Piano

_____ 5. Speaking French

_____   6. How to Stop Smoking

_____   7. Automobile Driving

_____   8. How I learned to speak English

_____   9. The English-English Dictionary

_____   10. Everything You've Always Wanted to Know About Using A Ski Lift in the Mountains

_____   11. A Cultural Experience: Shopping in a Super Market

_____   12. The Recent Politics of Malaysia

_____   13. OPEC

_____   14. Thailand's Progressive Educational System

_____   15. A Short History

REVISION EXERCISE 2   Following Directions

Read the process composition that follows: Revise this student composition by following directions at the end.

Hanging Things on Walls

(1)There is nothing more frustrating than to hang a picture over the sofa and, as you step back to look at it, the picture crashes to the floor. (2)Of course, not all pictures come down that quickly. (3)Some wait until you have guests, or they may come down in the middle of the night to scare everyone. (4)These disasters don't have to happen.

(5)Only two pieces of equipment are needed for this process: a lightweight hammer and the proper picture nail. (6)It is necessary to know what type of wall construction the picture will be hung on, because the wall construction determines the type of nail.

(7)Inspect the wall on which you plan to hang the picture. Most walls today are hollow, dry-wall construction. (8)If you drive a plain nail into this material, the wallboard will crumble and the weight of the picture will gradually pull the nail out. (9)For this type of wall, you need a hanger that has a nail and a flat piece on the outside that will help spread the weight. (10)Put the point against the wall where you want the picture to go and set the plate parallel with the wall. (11)Hammer the nail in gently and evenly.

(12)The other type of hanger consists of two pieces; the flat part of the hanger must line up with the wall, so that it rests against the wall when driven in.

1. Rewrite the title, so it is more specific.

2. Add a thesis sentence to the end of paragraph one.

3. Add a linking word or phrase before sentence 6.

4. Add a time order word or phrase before sentence 7.

5. Add time order words to sentences 10 and 11.

6. Add a conclusion that summarizes the steps and describes the results.

FOR WRITERS WHO HAVE MORE TO SAY

Journal Assignment

This chapter begins with a joke about a mother mouse and a cat. Can you recall a favorite joke? Record this joke in your journal and tell why you think it is funny.

Then discuss the following questions. Is humor the same in every culture? Have you noticed differences between the humor of your country and funny stories in American culture? Do yo think the humor in British culture is different from American humor?

Class Assignment

Choose one of these topics for a process composition of two to three pages:

How to Make the Most Popular Food in My Country

How to Pack a Suitcase

How to Learn about a New Culture

How to Select a New Car

How to Get an "A" in Writing Class

CHAPTER SUMMARY

There are two types of process compositions: one that explains or analyzes a process and one that instructs or directs readers how to follow a process.

A good process composition must be clear and specific and it must follow logically ordered steps.

In a process composition two things are important:

linking words that mark time and sequence, plus sentences that combine ideas to show relationships between one event and another.

A good title for a process composition, or any other type of writing, should be short, specific, and properly capitalized. Articles, prepositions, and conjunctions, unless they are the first word, should not be capitalized.

CHAPTER 8

Nothing Is Real but Hunger

Nothing is real to us but hunger.

—Maori Proverb

This young Ethiopian mother and child know nothing but the sadness of hunger. African children have suffered more than anyone. In Sudan, in 1984, almost 700,000 children died from starvation. In more recent years, millions have died as famine has swept other sub-Saharan countries.

Famine is a long food shortage that causes widespread hunger and death. Famine is an important world problem to analyze. What are its causes? What effects does it have on individuals? On nations?

JOURNAL ASSIGNMENT

A good way to become more fluent in writing is to freewrite (See page 18). A good place to do this freewriting is in your journal. Think about the proverb from the Maoris of New Zealand. What do you think this old saying means to the people of this land? What does the saying mean to you? What ideas do you have about the causes and effects of hunger?

USING THE WRITING PROCESS TO SHOW CAUSE AND EFFECTS

When writers analyze a problem, they discuss the relationships between causes and effects. They also may suggest solutions to the problem. The cause-effect pattern of writing is common in the American college or university classroom because it is a method to explain the "hows," or reasons, for particular events, beliefs, attitudes, and behaviors.

Finding out reasons is an important part of American culture. Looking at effects of an event, belief, attitude, or behavior also is important in American writing. If writers are more interested in effects than causes, they will explain "what will happen" or "what has happened" as the result of an event, belief, attitude, or behavior.

Questions writers ask to find out cause-effect relationships:

What causes _____ now? What caused it in the past? What may cause it in the future?

What are the results (consequences) of _____?

What is the effect of _____ on human beings, nature, countries, the world?

The best way to understand cause-effect writing is to practice it as we use the writing process.

GETTING IDEAS AS A GROUP

Famine is an important topic for a cause-effect composition. What causes this terrible food shortage that leads to the deaths of thousands, even millions, of

167

people? Spend 10–15 minutes discussing the causes of famine as a class or in small groups. Share ideas you have gained from your freewriting exercise. It may help to see the relationship between the topic and its causes, if ideas are put into a "web" pattern something like this:

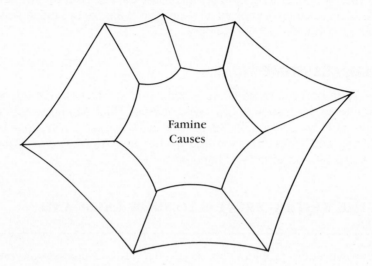

During the 10–15 minute discussion, try to focus only on causes. The effects of famine will be added to the web later.

FOR CLASS DISCUSSION

1. How many causes did the class discover?

2. What are they? Are any of them related to one another? Which ones?

3. What, in your opinion, is the major cause of famine?

ADDING TO IDEAS BY READING

Because famine is an issue in today's world, we have ideas and opinions about it, but in order to write intelligently we should add to our opinions by gaining some factual information. The encyclopedia is a helpful set of books to use for general information and background about a topic.

Read the following article from *World Book Encyclopedia,* 1986, about the causes of famine. This article will give you additional information from which to write.

Drought ranks as the chief cause of famine. Certain regions of China, India, and Russia have always been those hardest hit by famine. All three have large areas, near deserts, where rainfall is light and variable. In a dry year, crops in those areas fail and famine may strike. In the 1870's, for example, dry weather in the Deccan plateau of southern India caused a famine that took about 5 million lives. During the same period, a famine in China killed more than 9 million persons.

In the late 1960's and early 1970's, lack of rain produced widespread famine in a region of Africa called the Sahel. The estimated number of deaths was about a million. The Sahel lies just south of Sahara. It includes parts of Chad, Mali, Mauritania, Niger, Senegal, the Sudan, Upper Volta, and other nations. Famine struck the Sahel again in the early 1980's.

Too much rainfall may also bring famine. Rivers swollen by heavy rains overflow their banks and destroy farmland. Other crops rot in the field because of the excess water. . . .

Plant diseases and pests sometimes produce famine. During the 1840's a plant disease destroyed most of Ireland's potato crop. Between 1841 and 1851, Ireland's population dropped by about 2 ½ million persons through starvation, disease, and emigration.

Other causes of famine include both natural and human ones. Such natural disasters as cyclones, earthquakes, early frosts, and tidal waves may affect a large area, destroying enough crops to create a famine. War may result in a famine if many farmers leave their fields and join the armed forces. In some cases, an army has deliberately created a famine to starve an enemy into surrender. The army destroys stored food and growing crops and sets up a blockade to cut off the enemy's food supply. Blockades prevented shipments of food from reaching Biafra during the Nigerian Civil War (1967–70). A famine resulted, and more than a million Biafrans probably starved.

Notice how the following words were used in the article on famine and discuss the meaning and usage of these words with your instructor and classmates.

drought	swollen
variable	deliberately
crops	blockage
widespread	starved
emigration	

EXERCISE 8-1   **Taking Notes in Preparation to Write**

Skim the article again and take notes in the outline form that follows. Some of the topics in the outline have been filled in to guide you.

Causes of Famine

I. Drought

   A. China, India, and Russia in the 1870s

   B. _____

II. _____

   A. Rivers flood and destroy farms.

   B. _____

III. _____

IV. _____

   A. _____

      1. _____

      2. _____

      3. _____

      4. _____

   B. Human

      1. Farmers leave fields to join army.

      2. _____

QUESTIONS FOR CLASS DISCUSSION

1. What are the causes of famine listed in the outline?
2. Can a particular famine have more than one cause? Explain.
3. What do you think caused the recent famines in African countries?
4. Has your country ever experienced any of the causes of famine? Which one? When?
5. Were any of the causes discussed in the article the same ones you discovered as a class?

FOCUS AND SUPPORT

Look over your outline (Exercise 8-1) with the purpose of writing a statement about the causes of famine. Write two possible main idea sentences:

1. _____

2. _____

Choose the best of these two statements as the first sentence of a paragraph that summarizes the causes of famine. Use your outline but do **not** look back at the encyclopedia article. Your paragraph should be from 6 to 10 sentences in length.

   When you have finished writing, read your paragraph to check for clearness of ideas. Have you included the four major divisions of the outline? Is your first sentence supported by all the other sentences?

   Keep this paragraph. You will use it as part of a longer composition.

SMALL GROUP EXERCISE

Now that you know and have written about the causes of famine, it is important to discuss the **effects** of this problem. In small groups of three to four persons, discuss what possible results (effects) come from the situation of famine in a country.

   One person in the group may wish to record the effects in a web pattern similar to the one that follows. To guide the group's discussion, answer these questions:

   What are the effects of famine on individuals?

   What are the effects on a country?

   What are the effects on a region of the world?

   What are the effects of famine in terms of physical environment? (Living conditions in homes, towns)

   What are the effects of famine in terms of emotional environment? (Family relationships, happiness, anger, friendship)

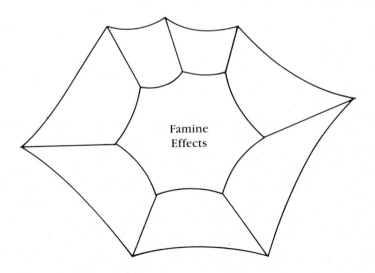

Famine
Effects

After spending 5–10 minutes recording effects, look over the web pattern. With your group, decide what are the four most important effects of famine. Circle these on the pattern.

Report back to the class on your group's discussion. A tally of group opinion may be taken to find out the four major effects as decided by the class. Record the results here:

The four major effects of famine:

1. _____

2. _____

3. _____

4. _____

WRITING THE SECOND PARAGRAPH

Now, as a group, with the instructor as recorder on the blackboard, write a paragraph about the major effects of famine.

Begin with a main idea sentence that states the major effects.

Support this main idea with a brief discussion of each effect.

Finish with a sentence that either summarizes the effects or states an attitude toward them.

To participate in a blackboard composition, you should suggest possible sentences to the instructor, who records them on the blackboard. After a sentence is recorded, you or other students may suggest changes in the sentence or continue with other sentences. After the paragraph is finished, review it and make revisions.

When the revised paragraph is ready, make corrections in grammar, punctuation, and spelling.

Is the blackboard composition complete? If so, record it in your notebook for use in the next exercise.

EXERCISE 8-2   Combining Paragraphs into a Longer Composition

By adding an introduction, a few linking words, and a conclusion, you will have a full-length composition about famine.

Follow these steps:

1. Write several sentences to introduce the topic of famine. You may wish to define the word *famine* (see the beginning of this chapter) and then to comment on its seriousness in the world today or on its appearance throughout history.

2. Add your first paragraph about the causes of famine. In order to make this paragraph fit smoothly with your introduction, you may need to add a sentence that states that there usually is more than one cause behind famine.

3. Next add the paragraph that you wrote about the effects of famine. If necessary, add a linking word or phrase before the paragraph to make a smooth transition from causes to effects.

4. Add one or two concluding sentences that make a general statement about famine which you believe to be true. These sentences could focus on the seriousness of famine as a world problem or on the need for all countries to work toward preventing famine.

5. Read aloud your entire composition. Make revisions and rewrite if necessary.

WORDS AND PHRASES THAT SHOW CAUSE AND EFFECT

as a result	*As a result* of no rain, farmers' crops are ruined. Farmers' crops are ruined *as a result* of no rain.
as a consequence	*As a consequence* of famine, the next generation of children will suffer poor health. The next generation of children will suffer poor health *as a consequence of famine.*
and so	Plant diseases can cause famine, *and so* it is necessary to prevent these diseases.
one reason for	*One reason for* famine is too much rainfall.
consequently	It is the poor who suffer most from famine; *consequently,* rich leaders sometimes do not pay attention to the problem.
therefore	The army wanted to starve their enemy into surrendering; *therefore,* they destroyed food supplies. The army wanted to starve their enemy into surrendering. They *therefore* destroyed food supplies.
and that is why	During the 1870s in China, there was a very bad drought, *and that is why* the rice crops failed.
because of	*Because of* the Chinese famine, more than 9 million people died. More than 9 million people died *because of* the Chinese famine.
because	*Because* people in the world were concerned about the lives of Ethiopians, they donated billions of dollars. People in the world donated billions of dollars *because* they were concerned about the lives of Ethiopians.

thus   The Deccan plateau of southern India has dry weather and desert conditions; *thus,* it is a probable place for famine.

The Deccan plateau of southern India has dry weather and desert conditions. *Thus,* it is a probable place for famine.

hence   Proper diet is necessary for the growth of children; *hence,* famine slows that growth.

Proper diet is necessary for the growth of children. *Hence,* famine slows that growth.

As you can see from the examples, cause or effect words are like signposts that tell the reader the relationship between ideas. Many of the words and phrases can be used either to begin a sentence or to connect parts of a sentence. The exercises that follow will give you practice in using the words and phrases in the list.

EXERCISES TO POLISH UP YOUR WRITING

EXERCISE 8-3   Using Cause and Effect Words and Phrases

All of the items in this exercise are about cities and their advantages and problems. Read each sentence and choose a word or phrase from the previous list to fill the blank. Use the example in the list as a pattern for the correct punctuation and use of the word or phrase. Use a different word or phrase for each sentence.

1. Many people like to live in a big city _____ the variety of entertainment offered there.

2. _____ many businesses and industries, people move to the big cities to find work.

3. Large cities usually have among their citizenry many poor people _____ there are problems with housing and jobs.

4. _____ pollution is the number of industries in many large cities.

5. The great number of automobiles driven in the city emit exhaust fumes _____ there is a pollution problem.

6. The crime rate is higher in large cities _____ the

   need for a strong police force.

7. Life is complicated and fast _____ stress is

   another problem of city living.

8. New York is an exciting city _____ museums,

   universities, theatres, restaurants, and large stores.

9. Parking is expensive and difficult to find _____

   many people use buses and subways for transportation.

10. _____ office space is expensive, many large

    businesses are moving to the suburbs.

11. City government must provide many services for its population

    _____ taxes usually quite high.

12. _____ not enough jobs for those who need

    them, unskilled people are unhappy with city life.

13. People of many different minorities travel to the city

    _____ the hope of finding work.

14. _____ it is truly a melting pot of cultures, I like a

    big city better than a small town.

15. _____ preferring life in a small town is that day-

    to-day living is simpler and less stressful.

TRANSITIONS BETWEEN RELATED SENTENCES

The linking expressions used in Exercise 8-3 provide transitions between two complete sentences or two independent clauses. These words include.

> *thus   therefore   consequently   as a result   for this reason*

These linking expressions must be preceded by either a period or a semicolon. They cannot be preceded by a comma, but a comma often follows them.

EXAMPLES

Life is complicated and fast; *thus,* stress is another problem of city-living.

The country of Oman has both mountains and deserts; *therefore,* it is a land of great variety.

DDT reduced the mosquito population. *Consequently,* the problem of malaria was lessened.

Maria never ate fruit or drank juices. *As a result,* she had a vitamin C deficiency.

It rained heavily for six days. *For this reason,* the roof of the house was leaking badly.

These words also can be used within an independent clause. When used this way, they are set off by commas.

EXAMPLE

It had rained heavily for six days. The roof of the house, *for this reason,* was leaking badly.

EXERCISE 8-4   Using Linking Expressions Between Sentences

Finish each idea with a sentence that begins with one of these linking expressions: *thus, therefore, consequently, as a result, for this reason.*

EXAMPLE

George stayed up all night studying _____

George stayed up all night studying; *therefore,* he fell asleep during the test.

All of the sentences in this exercise are about Live Aid, the biggest rock-and-roll concert in history. The concert was given in July 1985 in both London and Philadelphia. More than a billion and a half people in 160 countries may have watched the concert on TV. The purpose of Live Aid was to raise money for the starving people in Africa. People who watched the concert on TV donated money and those who watched it live bought tickets, money from which went to Africa.

1. Thousands of young people wanted to see and hear in person the famous

   rock stars _____

   _____

2. Americans paid $35 for seats _____

   _____

3. Fifty million dollars was raised by the concert _____

   _____

4. Many satellites were used to broadcast the concert _____

   _____

5. A terrible drought swept Africa during late 1984 and 1985 _____

   _____

6. JFK Stadium in Philadelphia holds 10,000 people _____

   _____

7. The concert was 16 hours long _____

   _____

8. People who watched the concert really wanted to help starving Africans __

   _____

9. The concert helped people all over the world to find out about the famine in

   Africa _____

   _____

COMBINING SENTENCES TO SHOW RELATIONSHIPS

Exercise 8-4 showed that short sentences can be combined to clearly show the
relationship between cause and effect. However, sometimes when a writer is think-

ing about two related ideas, it is difficult to tell which is the cause and which is the effect. This short definition may help:

> **A cause is a connection between events that lets us say: without event A, event B would not have come about, or whenever you have A you will have B.**

The following exercise will give you practice in identifying the cause and the effect and in combining sentences with cause-effect transitions.

EXERCISE 8-5 Sentence Combining

Read each pair of sentences. Decide which is the cause sentence and which is the effect. Mark *C* (cause) or *E* (effect) in the blank to the left of each sentence. (If this seems difficult, ask yourself "what comes first?" The answer will be the cause.)

Next, combine the two sentences on the blank beneath. Use words listed on pages 173–174. Try not to use the same linking word more than once. Be certain to put the cause sentence **after** the effect when using *because, since, consequently, therefore,* and *that is why.*

EXAMPLE

_*E*_ The food supply in poor and rich countries differs greatly.

_*C*_ There are differences in farm output in the poor countries and the rich countries.

> Combined: The food supply in poor and rich countries differs greatly *because* of differences in farm output.

_____ 1. No one can live without food.

_____ The supply of food always has been a main concern of man.

_____

_____ 2. The world's food supply changes from year to year.

_____ The production of crops and animals changes.

_____

_____ 3. The world's population grows every year.

_____ The worldwide demand for food increases.

_____

_____ 4. Famines happen.

_____   The food supply falls short of the amount needed.

_____

_____ 5. Most people in developed countries have an adequate diet.

_____   Almost all developed countries are in parts of the world suitable for

           farming.

_____

_____ 6. Developed countries have enough food.

_____   Their populations grow more slowly than their food supply.

_____

_____ 7. Developing nations often do not have enough food.

_____   Developing nations are in or near the tropics and not suited to heavy

           production of food.

_____

_____ 8. Developing nations have too little food.

_____   The population grows nearly as fast, or faster than, their food sup-

           ply.

_____

VERB TENSES AND CAUSE-EFFECT ANALYSIS

When analyzing events in general, such as war, crime, famine, and so on, we use simple present tense. Use of this tense tells the reader that we are talking about events that happen in a regular pattern, in other words, habitual or customary events.

EXAMPLE

　　War *is* hell.

Crime *is* common in big cities.

When analyzing a specific event, such as World War II, a robbery committed last week, or the Ethiopian famine in 1984–85, we use simple past tense to indicate that the event happened at a definite time in the past.

EXAMPLE

World War II *caused* the American people to show loyalty to this country.

The Ethiopian famine *resulted* in the deaths of millions of people.

EXERCISE 8-6   Recognizing Correct Verb Tenses

Read the paragraph below. It discusses automobile accidents in general and one accident in particular. Underline each verb. Correct the verb tense if necessary.

Automobile Accidents

More than 18 million auto accidents happened in the United States every

year. These accidents cause the deaths of 46,000 persons and injure about

3 1/2 million people yearly. Drinking was a major cause of driving errors that

result in serious accidents. A good example of the carelessness of American

drivers is the three-car accident that happen last Saturday on the highway near

the university. Three people were killed because of the reckless driving of a

young man who is drinking and driving without a license. This accident is just

one of thousands that are caused by drunk drivers. I believe we needed stricter

laws against drinking while driving.

READING A GRAPH TO GAIN INFORMATION

Many times when writers analyze the causes or the effects of a situation, they need to use facts that are presented in the form of a graph or table. The following exercise will give you practice in gathering information from a graph.

EXERCISE 8-7 **Information from a Graph**

The graph below shows the percentage contributions to world food production and world population of each of the major world regions.

The first bar represents the percentage of world food produced by that area of the world, and the second bar represents the percentage of world population living in that area.

Study the graph and complete the sentences that follow.

ııııı **Food Production** ■■■ **Population**

Asia ▲
ııııııııııııııııııııııııııııııı 35%
■■■■■■■■■■■■■■■■■■■■■■■■■■■■ 59%

Europe *
ıııııııııııııııııııııııııııııııı/ 33%
■■■■■■■ 17%

United States and Canada
ııııııııııııı 14%
■■■ 6%

Latin America
ıııııııııı 9%
■■■■ 9%

Africa
ııııııııı 8%
■■■■ 9%

Australia and New Zealand
ı 1%
▪ Less than 1%

0   10   20   30   40   50   60
Percentage of World Total

▲ Including Asian Russia
* Excluding Asian Russia
Source: Production Yearbook 1980, FAO. Figures are for 1980.

The relation between food production and population.

1. Asia produces 35% of the world's food, but it has _____ of

   the world's population.

2. Europe contributes _____ of the world's food, which is

almost more than _____ what it needs to feed its population.

3. The United States and Canada produce 14% of _____ but have only _____ of its population.

4. Latin America produces _____ of the world's food, exactly enough to feed _____ of its population.

5. Africa produces _____ and has _____.

6. Asia, Africa, and Latin America have over _____% of the world's people but produce only about _____% of its food.

EXERCISE 8-8   Writing a Paragraph from Data

The graph that you studied for Exercise 8-7 shows the relationship between the amount of food produced in an area and the number of people that food must feed. How important is the relationship between food produced in an area and the number of people living there? Why? Answer this question in a complete sentence:

It is extremely important that _____

_____

        Which areas of the world do not produce enough food for their population? Why is this a problem? Answer these questions in a complete sentence:

_____

_____

        Now choose one of the sentences above as the main idea for a paragraph of 7–10 sentences. Support the main idea with information from the graph and the answers to Exercise 8-7. Follow the writing process to create a strong paragraph.

EXERCISE 8-9   More Practice Writing Cause-and-Effect

In this exercise, you will be asked to analyze a common campus problem: not enough parking spaces on campus for the number of students. The purpose of the analysis is to gather enough information and ideas to write a letter to the editor of the college newspaper. This letter will analyze the causes of the parking problem and suggest possible ways of solving it. The letter must be no more than 250 words in length.

The exercise will take you through the steps in the writing process that lead to the completed letter.

Step 1: Becoming Acquainted with the Problem

When a writer is given a topic he isn't familiar with, the writer must find out the facts about the topic before he can analyze it. To help you understand the problem, read the facts that follow and study the map of the campus.

Facts About Parking on the Campus of Southwest Community College

Southwest Community College has grown very rapidly in the 10 years since it was founded. It is located in a busy suburb of a major city. Only two major buildings are located on the campus, the North Building and the Main Classroom Building. The campus is bounded on the west by a heavily traveled interstate highway, on the east by railroad tracks, on the north by small businesses, and to the south by apartment buildings.

Since Southwest is a community college, many of its students work and attend classes; therefore, classes are offered heavily in the mornings and in the early evenings. The following are examples of the numbers of students attending classes at particular times of the day.

Monday-Wednesday-Friday Classes

　　8–12 A.M.: 2,500 students

　　1–5 P.M.: 1,000

　　6–8 P.M.: 1,000

Tuesday-Thursday Classes

　　8–12 A.M.: 1,500 students

　　1–5 P.M.: 500

　　6–8 P.M.: 1,000

As you can see, many of the required classes are offered in the mornings on Monday, Wednesday, and Friday; so parking problems are especially bad at these times.

Students do not have to pay for parking on campus. There are only three lots to choose from. Two of the lots north of the main building are marked with white lines that allow enough space for a large car to park comfortably. The other lot is unmarked. Problems that are related to lack of parking include students coming late to morning classes because they cannot find a place to park, local businesses and apartments complaining about students parking illegally in their lots, and instructors complaining about the fact that they do not have a reserved area set aside for staff parking.

SOUTHWEST COMMUNITY COLLEGE

Step 2   Analyzing the Problem for its Causes

This step is the same as "Getting Ideas," a first step that you have followed in other chapters. In this assignment, you will get ideas about the causes of Southwest College's parking problems.

It will be helpful to form a small group of two to three students to discuss the causes. One student can record suggestions on the web pattern that follows:

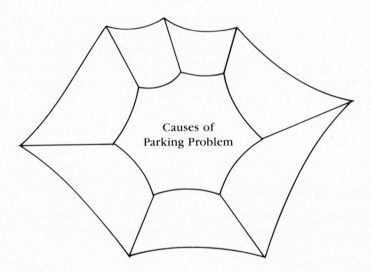

Causes of
Parking Problem

After each group has analyzed the parking problem to determine its causes, come together as a total class to share ideas that you have recorded as groups.

Record the major ideas gathered by the class. Rank them in order of importance.

Causes of Southwest College's Parking Problem

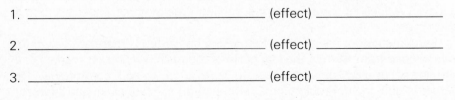

1. _____ (effect) _____

2. _____ (effect) _____

3. _____ (effect) _____

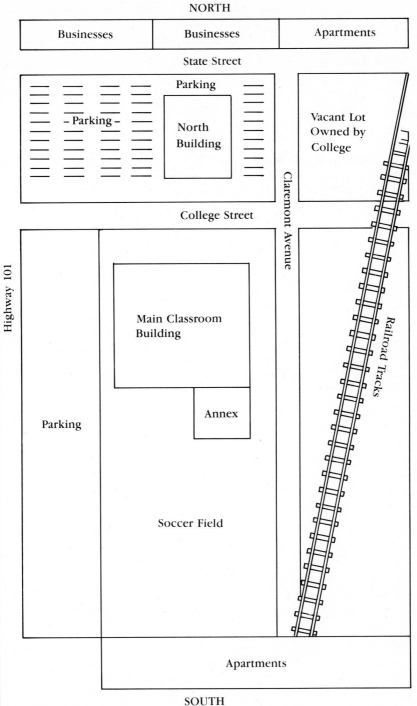

4. _____ (effect) _____

5. _____ (effect) _____

As a group you also may wish to explore the effects of each cause. For example, if you listed "no lines marked in west lot" as one of the causes, the effect of that cause would be "some cars take up too much space or park unevenly, so the parking area is not efficiently used."

Step 3   Focusing on Major Causes of the Problem

What are the major causes of Southwest College's parking problem? State your answer in a complete sentence that includes the topic (Southwest College's parking problem).

Possible Focus: _____

_____

_____

Since part of your task is to consider possible solutions, it is a good idea now to get ideas about those solutions. List those ideas here after looking back at the causes and effects of the problem.

Possible Solutions to the Parking Problem

1. _____

2. _____

3. _____

4. _____

5. _____

Which of the solutions listed above seem to be the best ways to solve the problem? Circle the numbers.

Write a statement that gives the answer to the problem?

Possible Focus: _____

_____

_____

Now you're faced with the task of combining your attitude toward the causes of the parking problem and its possible solution. Since a letter to the editor needs to be very direct and rather short, you need to write a thesis statement that says both something about the causes and something about the solutions. You may put this attitude into one or two sentences.

Possible Thesis for Letter to Editor: _____

_____

_____

Step 4   Supporting Your Thesis

Read your thesis statement again. Look back at the previous ideas you gathered and the information about parking on campus. Take notes on the ideas that will strongly support your thesis. Remember that your audience is mainly college students like yourself and a few instructors who read the campus newspaper. What ideas will make these readers agree with you?

Step 5   Drafting

Write a rough draft of your letter to the editor. These hints may help you in drafting:

1. Begin the letter with *Dear Editor:*

2. Since your space is limited, it isn't necessary to write an introductory sentence. However, if you wish to begin with a general introduction that states something about the seriousness of the problem, keep this introduction to one sentence.

3. The editor is a student and so are the majority of your readers. Keep this in mind when you choose vocabulary for the composition. Also remember that students know the layout of the campus and have experienced the problem; therefore, you don't need to waste valuable space describing where the lots are or discussing how difficult it is to park. Be direct and to the point.

4. After you have discussed your solution to the parking problem, end the letter with a sentence that refers back to your original thesis.

5. Close the letter in the following manner:

> Sincerely,
> Nadia Ghanem
> Southwest College Student

Step 6   Revising and Drafting Again

1. Read the letter aloud, asking yourself these questions:

    Is the thesis clear and understandable?

Does everything else in the letter support the thesis?

Did I conclude the letter with a sentence that restates the thesis?

Is the vocabulary appropriate for my readers—other college students and some instructors?

Did I speak directly to these readers?

2. Make changes in organization before considering changes in grammar, spelling, and punctuation. Consult your editing checklist on page 243.

3. Exchange letters with another student in class. Read that student's letter· and answer the questions asked above. Make suggestions and return the letter to the student.

4. Use this feedback to help you make changes and corrections. In other words, draft the letter a final time.

WRITING CONCLUSIONS

The purpose of a conclusion is to make the idea of the composition stronger and to leave the reader with a feeling of completion. Not all compositions need separate concluding paragraphs. Short narrative and descriptive compositions will probably not need concluding paragraphs, nor will one- to two-page essays in which the reader can easily remember everything you have written. Sometimes a strong final sentence or two can often serve as well as a separate paragraph.

If you do need a conclusion to tie your main points together and leave the reader with a sense of unity, you may wish to use some of these ideas.

End by referring to your thesis statement, or restating it in different words.

If the world is to become a peaceful place, hunger is a challenge that every nation, rich or poor, must face.

The thesis sentence for this short composition was "Although hunger may occur in countries other than our own, it is a problem that all nations must confront and solve."

End with a quotation.

In most modern American marriages, both husband and wife work outside the home. However, most homes and places of work are still organized as if only the husbands work. According to Betty Friedan, author of several women's rights books, "Jobs are still structured for men whose wives take care of the details of life, and homes are still structured for women whose only responsibility is running their families."

End with a short one- or two-sentence summary.

In short, my mother not only cares for her family, but for her neighbors and needy strangers as well.

End by looking to the future.

If the problem of hunger in Africa is not solved in this decade, what will be the result in 10 or 20 years? In my opinion, the death of a whole generation of Africans will occur if all of us do not help solve the problem.

End by calling for action.

As one can see, gun control is an absolute necessity if we are going to end the senseless killing that takes place everyday. If we act now, by writing to our senators and representatives and convincing our friends that handguns should be illegal, we may prevent the deaths of hundreds of people.

EXERCISE 8-10   Writing Conclusions

The letter that follows is about a problem on campus. It does not have a conclusion. Read the letter and write five different conclusions for it. Each conclusion need be only one or two sentences in length.

Dear Editor:

One of the major problems on this campus is the lack of student advisors who really care about the academic concerns of students. In my 1 ½ years as a student at Southwest, I have never been able to arrange more than a 5-minute session with an advisor in my major. On the few occasions I have been able to find the advisor, his approach was: "Look at the course requirements and sign up for the classes you need." My questions about advantages of one class over another, career opportunities in the field, and the possibility of an internship went unanswered. The advisor either didn't know the answers or didn't care about helping me.

I am not alone in this problem. My friends in this major and in other areas have expressed the same concern.

1. Conclude by referring to the thesis statement: _____

_____

2. Conclude with a quotation. (This could be a quote from another student.):

_____

3. Conclude with a summary:_____

_____

4. Conclude by looking to the future:_____

_____

5. Conclude by calling for action:_____

_____

REVISION EXERCISES

REVISION EXERCISE 1   Making Changes in Organization

Some of the most important revisions happen when a writer checks the organization of his composition to see if he or she has analyzed causes and effects properly. The student outline that follows has some major problems in organization. Rewrite the outline so the causes of the problem and its solutions are divided into two clear-cut groups.

Thesis: The lack of parking on campus is a frustrating problem, with several causes, and three easy solutions.

Outline: Parking on Campus

I. Causes of the Parking Problem
    A. Too many classes scheduled in morning
    B. Parking lots too crowded
    C. All spaces need to be marked with lines
    D. Students park illegally in nearby businesses
II. Solutions to the Parking Problem
    A. Schedule popular classes all throughout the day
    B. Use undeveloped east area for another lot
    C. Everyone drives a car rather than taking public transportation.
    D. Parking space is free on campus but not free off campus

REVISION EXERCISE 2   Smoothness and Clarity

Read this letter to the editor of the college newspaper; then, make the revisions suggested below the letter. Rewrite the letter in correct form.

Dear Editor:

[1]I would like to urge all international students to vote for Munim Abdullah for president of the International Student Association. [2]He has three years of experience in the student senate. [3]He has learned about the problems of international students on this campus. [4]Munim is acquainted with students from every culture, not just those from his own country. [5]He knows most of these students by name and is really concerned about them. [6]He has lived in the dormitory since he entered the university. [7]He knows American students, too. [8]Munim's major is international relations, which provides excellent background for the position of International Student president.

[9]Don't forget to vote for Munim Abdullah for ISA president.

Sincerely,

Moon Seok

1. Combine sentences 2 and 3 to show cause-effect relationship.

2. Use a transition in front of sentence 4 to show that this is another qualification of Munim's.

3. Replace the *and* in sentence 5 with a word that shows "knows most of these students by name" is an effect of "is really concerned."

4. Combine sentences 6 and 7 to show cause-effect.

5. Use a transition before sentence 8 to show that this is the final qualification mentioned in the letter.

FOR WRITERS WHO HAVE MORE TO SAY

Journal Assignment

Is there something you have always been afraid of? In your journal, explore the causes of this fear. Does the fear have any effects on your life? Discuss these.

Class Assignment

Write a fully developed essay of three to five paragraphs on one of these topics:

The positive effects of having international students on an American college or university campus.

Reasons for choosing your major

Effects of smoking on your health and the health of those around you

The causes and effects of a problem in your country (pollution, lack of jobs, threat of war, and so on).

CHAPTER SUMMARY

When writers analyze a problem, they discuss the relationship between causes and effects. Cause-effect compositions can be developed through sharing opinions with a group, but it is also necessary to use factual information from reference books and other library sources.

As in all writing, linking expressions are important to the smoothness and clarity of a cause-effect essay. Words such as *therefore, consequently, as a result, for this reason,* and *thus* can be used to provide transitions between two complete sentences or two independent clauses.

Conclusions should make the idea of a composition stronger and leave the reader with a feeling of completion. Five possible conclusions include:

Referring to the thesis

Quotation

Short one- or two-sentence summary

Looking to the future

Calling for action

CHAPTER 9
Saying What We Feel

Let us say what we feel.

—Seneca

JOURNAL ASSIGNMENT

Do you say what you feel? Sometimes it is easier to write what you feel and by writing, you find that your beliefs are made clearer. As you work through this chapter, use your journal to record thoughts about your strongest beliefs and values. What do you value the most about life? Family? Religion? Political freedom? Education? What has caused you to have these values? Do you have strong opinions that have come from these values? What are your strongest opinions?

The notes in your journal are useful to you in two ways: you can learn more about yourself through these notes and you can get good ideas for additional writing in class.

USING THE WRITING PROCESS TO CONVINCE OR PERSUADE

One of the purposes of writing is to convince or persuade your readers to agree with your opinion, theory, or particular solution to a problem. Paragraphs and essays with this purpose are described as argument.

An argument must focus on an idea about which you can really argue. In other words, it must be an idea with two sides, one **for** and one **against.** For example, you cannot really argue about a statement such as: "The main crops grown in Malaysia are palm oil, copra, rice, and pepper." This is a statement of fact and does not have two opposing sides.

In the previous chapters you learned that the main idea of a paragraph is a topic sentence, and the main idea of an essay is a thesis sentence. In an argument, however, the main idea is called a proposition.

The **proposition** is the idea that you want your readers to agree with. To develop a good argument, you need to state the proposition clearly as one of the two sides of a topic. For example, what is your reaction to the photos of women naval officers at the beginning of this chapter? Do you believe that women should serve in the army or navy of a country? Why? Why not?

The topic of women's military service could become a proposition that would be the focus of an argument paragraph or essay. You may believe in women soliders or you may not. No matter what your opinion is, your position will be more convincing if it is supported with good reasons.

GROUP EXERCISE: GETTING IDEAS FOR AN ARGUMENT

Divide into groups of three or four students each. Half of the groups in class may take the position that agrees that "women should serve in the armed forces of a country." The other groups should take the opposing view "Women should not be allowed to serve in the armed forces of a country."

Each group should choose a person to write down ideas as they are discussed. Before you begin discussing reasons that support your side of the argument, talk about these three points:

1. How should we define "service in the armed forces"? Does this mean active service using weapons? Service as doctors, nurses, secretaries?

2. Should we limit our argument to certain women? Unmarried? Married? What age? Childless women?

3. How should we define "a country"? Does it matter which country?

After your group has agreed on answers to the questions above, discuss all possible reasons to support your side of the argument. At the end of your discussion (about 5–10 minutes) each member of the group may complete the statements that follow:

Thesis: In my opinion, women _____

_____

Our group definition of "service in the armed forces" is _____

_____.

Our group would limit "women" to those who are _____

_____,

in countries that _____.

These reasons support my opinion:

1. _____

2. _____

3. _____

As one can see from the above reasons, women _____

_____

You may wish to have an informal debate with groups on one side presenting reasons **for** women's service in the armed forces and other groups presenting reasons **against** this proposition.

WRITING AN ARGUMENT

The group discussion has given you some ideas about the topic of women in military service. You probably know which side of the argument you would choose to support. Your focus for a composition is the side that you wish to support. Since an argument requires more than one supporting idea to convince your readers, you will need more than one paragraph to develop your argument well.

The organization of your argument might follow this form:

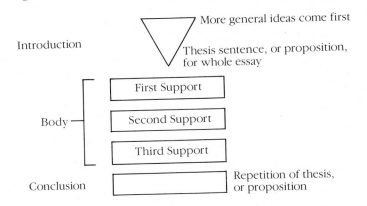

So far, in the essays you have written, you have not had a separate introductory paragraph and a separate conclusion. These two additional paragraphs are necessary for an argument essay. The **introductory paragraph** leads your readers into the topic and introduces them to your proposition (thesis). This paragraph, which begins generally and ends specifically, should make your readers want to continue reading. The **conclusion** is your opportunity to tie up the major points you have made and remind your readers of the proposition.

HOW TO BEGIN
Review the notes you made during the group discussion.

Which side of the argument can you support most strongly? State this side in a sentence.

Do you want to limit the age or status of women? Do you want to say how long they should serve? Are there any other ways you want to limit your argument? If so, add these limitations to the statement. (For example, I believe that single women between the ages of 18 and 25 should serve in the armed forces for a minimum of three years.)

The statement you have written is your proposition; it is the thesis of your whole essay.

Now list the three strongest reasons you have to support this proposition.

Think of an idea for the introductory paragraph.

1. You might begin by asking a question that will interest your readers and make them want to read on.

2. You can begin with a little story or anecdote that will catch your readers' interest.

3. You may begin with a fact about women's abilities, about the numbers of women in the military, or about military service in your own country.

Your thesis sentence, or proposition, will follow the sentences of introduction. In other words, this thesis statement will be the last sentence of the introductory paragraph.

Consider how you wish to conclude the essay.

The conclusion is your last chance to convince your readers to believe as you do. Here are some ideas:

1. Begin the final paragraph with a question. Answer the question with a summary of points included in the body of the essay.

2. Stress the need for concern about the topic and why readers should be concerned about women and military service.

3. Summarize the main supporting points.

No matter what type of conclusion you choose, don't forget to end with the thesis sentence, or proposition, of the whole essay. Word this sentence a bit differently than you did in the first paragraph.

USING A FORMAL OUTLINE

Formal outlines are helpful to use as guides when you write. However, it is best to generate ideas, focus on a thesis, and think about your support before writing the outline. Outlines can be used as a guide to writing or they can be used after you have written the rough draft to check for clear and logical organization.

EXERCISE 9-1 Writing a Formal Outline

Use the following blank pattern to outline your argument. If you have more than two points in any paragraph, add the necessary extra letters. Outlines should be either in phrases or complete sentences. Do not mix the two in the same outline.

Thesis Sentence: _____

_____

Title: _____

I. Introduction

    A. _____

    B. _____

II. _____

    A. _____

    B. _____

III. _____

    A. _____

    B. _____

IV. _____

    A. _____

    B. _____

V. _____

    A. _____

    B. _____

WRITING A ROUGH DRAFT OF YOUR ARGUMENT

Now it's time to put your pen to the paper; using your outline as a guide, write a rough draft of the five paragraphs. Do not worry about grammar, punctuation, and spelling. Simply try to get your thoughts on paper. It is much easier to revise and edit when you have your ideas written down.

    If possible, keep writing until you have finished each area of the outline— all five paragraphs. Then put aside the rough draft for several hours, or even overnight. A rough draft is like a cake that has just been taken from the oven. You can't decorate it or cut it until it cools.

    After the draft has "cooled," read it to see if there are weak spots. Answer these questions:

1. What do I like best about the essay?

2. Is the introduction interesting?

3. Did I clearly state my thesis, or proposition, at the end of the first paragraph?

4. Are the three supporting reasons clear and logical?

5. Do I need some more explanation of each reason? (In other words, are each of the supporting paragraphs detailed enough?)

6. Does the conclusion tie together my argument? Does it summarize the main points and remind readers of the original proposition?

Make necessary revisions and then share the draft with a classmate. After the classmate has read your essay, ask him or her the revision questions. Let the answers guide you in making any necessary revisions. Before submitting the essay to your instructor for suggestions, read through the next few pages to gain information about using facts in your argument.

USING FACTS FOR SUPPORT

In reviewing your rough draft, you may have found that you need more support for each of the reasons you have given. The best support for an argument is facts. Facts include data that have been proved and are generally accepted, such as facts from history, scientific data, and statistics. Getting facts may require some research in reference books or other library resources.

The Best Support for an Argument

Adequate evidence is really the only way to support and prove an argument. Adequate evidence is reliable, sufficient, and verifiable. Evidence is **reliable** if it comes from a source (person, book, magazine, reference work) that is trustworthy and informed. It is **sufficient** if there is enough of it to support all the points made in your argument. And it is **verifiable** if it is based on fact and not just opinion. Facts usually can be tested; opinion cannot. For example, the argument that there is a Loch Ness monster alive in Scotland cannot be proved—or disproved—because we don't have enough evidence. We lack reliable evidence because the trustworthiness of the people who say they have seen the monster is open to question. We lack sufficient evidence because very few people have reported seeing the monster, and many of these "viewings" have been connected with other causes. Finally, we lack verifiable evidence because we do not have a Loch Ness monster to examine.

Adequate Evidence

Using the Almanac for Facts

The **almanac** is a book of facts published each year. It includes facts about many topics, both in the United States and in other countries. Some of the topics are arts and media, nations of the world, U. S. presidents, trade and transportation, national defense, noted personalities, sports, astronomy, and hundreds of other topics.

The almanac has a **general index,** either at the front or back of the book, in which topics are listed alphabetically. For example, if you were looking for facts about military service, you would look in the *M*'s.

EXERCISE 9-2 Finding Facts in the Almanac

Reprinted here is a page from the index of *The World Almanac 1986*. Practice using this index by answering the questions that follow.

1. On what page would I find information about mineral production?

   _____

2. If I were writing about U. S. money, what page would give me facts? __

3. If I wanted information about the life of Mohamed, the prophet of Islam,

   where would I find it? _____

4. What three topics are found under *mining?* _____

   _____

5. If I were writing a paper about the number of ethnic groups in the state of

   Missouri on what page would I find these statistics? _____

6. If I were writing an argument about the benefits of buying foreign rather

   than U. S. cars, on what page would I find the comparison of mileage of

   new cars? _____

7. I want to support the proposition: *The minimum hourly wage in the United*

   States should be higher. Where would I find facts about minimum wages in

   the past 10 years? _____

8. On what page would I find the nutritive value of milk? _____

9. There are several listings under *Mississippi River.* Which listing would tell

   me about the business that is related to the river? _____

10. There are several listings under *military?* Which one would give me facts

    about the numbers of men and women in the military service? _____

_____

On what page is this listing? _____

EXERCISE 9-3   **Understanding Statistics**

To select the facts that will best support your argument, you must be able to
understand charts of statistics. Here is a chart from the almanac that shows
how many soldiers were in the army in various years from 1940 to 1985. The list
is divided to show total soldiers and to show men and women.
Examine the chart and answer the questions that follow.

U.S. Army
Source: Department of the Army
Army Military Personnel on Active Duty[1]

June 30[2]	Total strength	Commissioned officers Total	Male	Female[3]	Warrant officers Male[4]	Female	Enlisted personnel Total	Male	Female
1940	267,767	17,563	16,624	939	763	—	249,441	249,441	—
1942	3,074,184	203,137	190,662	12,475	3,285	—	2,867,762	2,867,762	—
1943	6,993,102	557,657	521,435	36,222	21,919	0	6,413,526	6,358,200	55,325
1944	7,992,868	740,077	692,351	47,726	36,893	10	7,215,888	7,144,601	71,287
1945	8,266,373	835,403	772,511	62,892	56,216	44	7,374,710	7,283,930	90,780
1946	1,889,690	257,300	240,643	16,657	9,826	18	1,622,546	1,605,847	16,699
1950	591,487	67,784	63,375	4,409	4,760	22	518,921	512,370	6,551
1955	1,107,606	111,347	106,173	5,174	10,552	48	985,659	977,943	7,716
1960	871,348	91,056	86,832	4,224	10,141	39	770,112	761,833	8,279
1965	967,049	101,812	98,029	3,783	10,285	23	854,929	846,409	8,520
1969	1,509,637	148,836	143,699	5,137	23,734	20	1,337,047	1,316,326	10,721
1970	1,319,735	143,704	138,469	5,235	23,005	13	1,153,013	1,141,537	11,476
1975	781,316	89,756	85,184	4,572	13,214	22	678,324	640,621	37,703
1978 (May 31)	772,202	96,553	90,749	5,804	13,160	57	662,432	614,961	47,471
1980 (Mar. 31)	762,739	83,117	76,237	6,880	13,093	103	666,426	608,223	58,203
1982 (Mar.)	788,026	87,874	79,379	8,495	14,058	143	685,951	618,783	67,168
1983 (Mar.)	774,704	89,012	80,091	8,921	14,481	178	674,033	606,956	67,077
1984 (Mar.)	774,935	90,393	81,046	9,347	14,971	198	669,373	602,702	66,67⁴
1985 (Mar.)	778,639	91,986	81,996	9,990	15,109	256	671,288	609,917	67,371

(1) Represents strength of the active Army, including Philippine Scouts, retired Regular Army personnel on extended active duty, and
National Guard and Reserve personnel on extended active duty; excludes U.S. Military Academy cadets, contract surgeons, and National
Guard and Reserve personnel not on extended active duty.
(2) Data for 1940 to 1947 include personnel in the Army Air Forces and its predecessors (Air Service and Air Corps).
(3) Includes: women doctors, dentists, and Medical Service Corps officers for 1946 and subsequent years, women in the Army Nurse
Corps for all years, and the Women's Army Corps and Women's Medical Specialists Corps (dieticians, physical therapists, and occupa-
tional specialists) for 1943 and subsequent years.
(4) Act of Congress approved April 27, 1926, directed the appointment as warrant officers of field clerks still in active service. Includes
flight officers as follows: 1943, 5,700; 1944, 13,615; 1945, 31,117; 1946, 2,580.

1. In what year was the army the largest? _____

2. How many women were in the army in 1943? _____

3. In what year was the army the smallest? _____

4. Using the answer to question 3, how many men were in the army? ____

   _____

5. Using the answer to question 3, how many women were in the army? _

   _____

6. How many women were in the army in 1984? _____

7. How many men were in the army during 1984? _____

8. What percentage of the 1984 total were women? _____

9. Can you use any of these facts to help support your argument about

   women in the armed services? _____

10. If yes, which facts? _____

Using Other Library References for Support

The almanac is an excellent resource for supporting facts for your argument. Other references, such as magazines, books, and encyclopedias can offer quotations from authorities, facts, history, and statistics that will help you support an argument.

Before finishing your argument paper, visit the library to search for some additional support.

EXERCISE 9-4   Using a Book for Support

In the card catalog, under *military service,* the following book was located: *Mixed Company: Women in the Modern Army* by Helen Rogan (New York: G. P. Putnam's Sons, 1981). Read the following excerpts and answer the questions at the end.

> There is no other country in the world in which women play such a large part in the uniformed military. There are only 10,000 female soldiers in the Russian armed forces of over four million. The armies of eastern and western Europe seem to have in common a lack of interest in expanding women's participation. Their governments apparently share the view expressed in confidential tones by a military attache at the British Embassy in Washington that Americans do take things too far.

American women are to be found on Navy vessels and on Air Force planes and training as astronauts, but the greatest concentration exists in the U. S. Army, where about 63,000 enlisted women and 4,000 officers live and work alongside men, in missile and helicopter repair, as tank-turret mechanics, and in the elite Old Guard, which participates in Washington ceremonials. They serve with the 82nd Airborne Division at Fort Bragg, they drive and service trucks, they train troops, male and female.

Approximately 28 out of 345 categories of work are closed to the women—the jobs in infantry, armor, cannon field artillery, combat engineering, and low-altitude air defense artillery. Any of these jobs would be likely to involve them in aggressive combat. Women are allowed into medium- and high-altitude air defense artillery jobs because missiles and rockets traveling at those altitudes are fired from far behind the front line. They can enter all aviation jobs except those of aerial scout and attack helicopter pilot. They can be every kind of medical specialist except a field medic, the person who literally crawls out onto the battlefield to tag or retrieve the wounded and dying (pp. 16–17).

. . . People have a moral twinge at the thought of women or thirteen-year-old boys or fifty-eight year old men going out to fight. We keep them out, which means we discriminate by sex and by age—*but we are keeping them out of the meat grinder.* What use is it to defend a nation that sends its women to the meat grinder? What are we defending? And what right do people have telling me I need to be resocialized, change my ideas? I say, Sez who, *and why are you so certain?* (Captain Edwards, U. S. Military Academy at West Point, p. 22).

1. The first paragraph includes facts about women in the U. S. military. Would these facts fit into your composition? If so, where in the composition would you put this information?

2. Paragraph 2 includes more facts about areas of the military in which women are involved. Which side of the argument could be best supported with these facts? (**For** women in the military or **against?**)

3. What is the main idea of paragraph 3? Which side of the argument could be well supported by this information?

4. What is the main idea of paragraph 4? Which side of the argument could be best supported by this quotation from Captain Edwards?

5. Finish the following statement by attaching it to the person and the book from which it was taken:
   "People have a moral twinge at the thought of women or thirteen-

   year-old boys or fifty-eight year old men going out to fight," _____

Telling Readers Where You Got Facts

If you borrow facts or quotations from library resources, you need to tell your readers where these references came from. In a more detailed essay, you would be required to formally document references, but for the purposes of this simplified essay, you need to connect that fact or quotation to a phrase that tells where it was found or who said it.

EXAMPLES

> More than 66,000 women were serving in the U. S. Army in 1984, according to *The World Almanac and Book of Facts, 1985.*

> "What sense does it make to kill a murderer to convince us that killing is morally and legally wrong?" asks Jim Sunderland of the Colorado Coalition Against the Death Penalty.

Notice that the title of a book (also of a magazine, encyclopedia, newspaper) is italicized in print. When you write a paper, you should underline those titles. Note also that a person's exact words are enclosed in quotation marks. More details about how to connect borrowed information to its source can be found on page 223 in the next chapter.

EXERCISE 9-5   Indicating Sources of Facts, Quotations

Write a sentence that includes the fact or quotation and also indicates the source for each of the numbered items that follow.

EXAMPLE

> We have a responsibility to act against terrorism. (Defense Secretary Caspar Weinberger *Newsweek,* June 7, 1981)

> "We have a responsibility to act against terrorism," stated Defense Secretary Caspar Weinberger in a June 1981 <u>Newsweek</u> interview.

1. It is the justice system's duty to do whatever is necessary to protect society. (Judge Douglas Wakeman)

_____

2. All OPEC nations in 1984 produced 17,575 barrels of oil per day. (*The World Almanac and Book of Facts, 1985*)

_____

3. In most instances, first-aid equipment aboard commercial aircraft in the U. S. is less than adequate. (Sheldon Shane, editor of *Travel-Holiday* magazine)

_____

4. Exercise increases the activity of interferon, which helps fight viruses. (a study by Italian scientists reported in the *Journal of Applied Physiology*)

_____

5. The diets of children with working mothers are just as nutritious as those of kids from "traditional" families. (a study done by MRCA Information Services)

_____

6. About 31% of old people in the United States live alone. (The Commonwealth Fund)

_____

7. Smokers need places to smoke. Even cockroaches have a place to go. (Senator Bob Martinez)

_____

8. Four percent of hospital admissions result from drug-induced illness. (*The People's Pharmacy,* a guide to prescription drugs)

_____

9. Cultural background is the single most powerful influence on our food likes and dislikes. (Psychologist Paul Rozin of the University of Pennsylvania)

_____

10. Americans watch more than 7 hours of TV everyday. (Television Bureau of Advertising)

_____

EXERCISES TO POLISH UP YOUR WRITING

Analyzing an Argument Essay

The following essay, written by a Japanese student studying English in the United States, argues that the Japanese emphasis on school exams must be changed. Read it and answer the questions that follow.

Mihoko Okura
Intermediate Writing
Professor Douglas
May 6, 1988

Examination Hell

   A 12-year-old student recently jumped to her death from an apartment building in northern Japan after she failed to pass a school examination. This incident is not unique. In 1983, 657 children under 20 took their lives in Japan, a 9.7% increase over the previous year. In addition, the child suicide rate in Japan is 2.6%, among the highest in the world, according to Todd Eastham, reporting for United Press International. From my point of view, these statistics clearly show that the system of school examinations in Japan must be changed.

   The major reason that changes must be made in the Japanese examination system is the mental and emotional stress that occurs because of the present system. "In this country only one entrance exam decides your career and how much advanced education you take," states Hirosi Azuma, dean of the University of Tokyo School of Education. The stress that results from these exams pushes some students to take their own lives and results in school violence in an otherwise largely nonviolent society. Even kindergarten students know that their parents are pushing them to pass tests to enter the best primary schools, so that they can then enter the best secondary schools, and finally make it into the best universities. This means a life of pressure to "be the best."

   In addition to promoting stress, the present system of education in Japan caters to the richer families who can provide tutoring and preparatory school fees that will give their children an advantage. "It has reached the point where to pass the entrance examination for the University of Tokyo, for example, you have to be also rich . . . which really defeats the purpose," Dean Azuma explains.

   The third reason for changing this system is that it does not teach students to solve problems, to really think. The "cram schools" that prepare students for testing just fill their heads with facts and figures rather than giving them real understanding. In my own experience, the cram school took 18 extra hours a week in addition to the regular six days of high school. I did this for one year before my entrance exam to just an average university. I passed the exam, but forgot all the facts promptly after the test was finished. I am convinced that this is not true education of the total person.

The percentage of students who pass their examinations to enter the best high schools and then the best universities have an open door to a life of opportunity, high salaries, and social status. The large percentage of students who fail have the door slammed in their faces, with no chance at good jobs, money, or position. This system creates stress that leads to suicide; it favors the wealthy families, and it does not provide a well-rounded education. For these reasons, I firmly believe that the system of school examinations in my country must be reformed.

1. What is the purpose of each of the paragraphs in Mihoko's essay?

2. How does she get the readers' attention in the introductory paragraph?

3. What is the thesis of her argument essay?

4. What are the three supporting reasons she gives for her proposition?

5. How does she conclude the essay? Does she restate her thesis in the same words as in the first paragraph?

6. There are at least 10 transition phrases and words that show strength of opinion, order of reasons, or additional support. Underline these in the essay.

7. Mihoko uses facts and quotations to explain her reasons. Find these and underline them.

8. The writer also uses personal experience to support her argument. Underline the personal experience she describes.

ADDING STRENGTH TO YOUR ARGUMENT

A writer can add strength to his argument by using words that show he believes strongly in his proposition. In the argument about Japanese exams, for example, the writer wrote "*I am convinced that* this is not true education. . . ."

The following words and phrases show strong belief:

I thoroughly approve/disapprove of

I completely agree/disagree with

I support/reject the idea that

I am certain that

I am convinced that

There is no question that

In my opinion,

Definitely

Undoubtedly

EXERCISE 9-6 Using Words and Phrases to Show Strength of Belief

Use each of the words and phrases listed above in a sentence that expresses your belief about the topics listed in this exercise.

EXAMPLE

influence of TV on children

I thoroughly disapprove of children watching unlimited hours of television.

1. medical care—government sponsored

_____

2. driving age

_____

3. women staying at home

_____

4. abortion

_____

5. unlimited immigration to the United States

_____

6. higher standards of English for international students entering U. S. universities

_____

7. no smoking in all public places

_____

8. U. S. military spending

_____

9. nuclear arms reduction between the United States and Russia

_____

10. second languages required for all American high-school students

_____

Words and Phrases that Show Additions

In writing an argument, you need to point out to your reader that you have more than one reason to support your proposition. This can be done by using words and phrases that remind the reader you are adding more facts or proof.

in addition	*In addition to* its harmful physical effects, alcohol can destroy personal relationships.
furthermore	*Furthermore,* alcohol is as habit forming as other hard drugs.
again	*Again,* let me emphasize the importance of fighting alcoholism.
besides	*Besides* being habit forming, alcohol is injurious to the physical body.
moreover	Alcoholism is a major American problem; *moreover,* it is a problem that must be solved if we are to maintain a quality life.
in fact	*In fact,* alcoholism is a problem all of us must tackle.
also	Alcoholism is a problem of mature adults; it is *also* a problem of teenagers.
as if that were not enough	Alcohol is physically harmful, addictive, and socially detrimental. *As if that were not enough,* it also has harmful effects on innocent people who are not alcoholics.

EXERCISE 9-7   **Using Words of Addition**

Use each of the eight words and phrases listed above in a sentence with the fact that is given in the exercise.

EXAMPLE

21,000 murders a year in the United States.

In addition, the United States has 21,000 murders a year.

1. an average of 5 persons executed each year in the United States.

_____

2. 10,000 homicides on TV or in movies each year

_____

3. shotguns in 26% of homes in this county

_____

4. rifles in 28%

_____

5. handguns in 21%

_____

6. Americans favor capital punishment

_____

7. weapons take lives of family members

_____

8. guns sold to anyone who wants to buy them

_____

REVISION EXERCISE

The argument paragraph that follows needs the addition of some linking words and phrases to improve clarity of ideas and coherence. Read the paragraph and answer the questions that follow.

Pets

(1)Sixty percent of all U. S. households include some kind of pet. (2)More than 40% of Americans have a dog, and more than 25% own a cat. (3)Pets, especially cats and dogs, are important in this high-tech society. (4)Every American home should have some kind of pet. (5)Pets give children the chance to take responsibility for caring for something other than themselves. (6)For those people who marry later, remain single or childless, a pet provides an outlet for their need to nurture. (7)A dog or cat also gives companionship to the many elderly people who live alone. (8)The responsive, loving traits of a pet offset the high technology in our lives.

1. Change the title to a few words that indicate the writer's attitude about pets.

2. Begin with a question that gets the reader's attention.

3. Add a phrase at the beginning of sentence 4 to state the firm belief of the writer. (This is the proposition sentence.)

4. Sentences 5, 6, and 7 present three reasons to have a pet. Begin each of these sentences with words that mark the steps (or additions) in the argument.

5. Add a linking word or phrase to sentence 8 to show that this is the final statement of the argument.

FOR WRITERS WHO HAVE MORE TO SAY

Journal Assignment

What are your opinions about the roles of men and women? In other words, are there clear-cut, well-defined activities that men should take part in? What are they? Do you want your spouse to follow the pattern that has been set in the past?

Class Assignment

Write a five-paragraph argument essay about one of these propositions:

1. There should be a nationwide law requiring seatbelts for all occupants of an automobile.

2. Commercial airlines should undergo more rigid safety inspections.

3. Governments that send students to the United States on scholarship should require them to major in areas needed to develop their countries.

4. Universities should lower the English proficiency requirements for international students.

5. The United States government should develop more peacetime uses of nuclear power.

CHAPTER SUMMARY

Writing with the purpose of convincing or persuading readers is called argument.

In an argument, the thesis is replaced by a similar statement that is called a proposition. The proposition states one side of a topic.

The five-paragraph essay practiced in this chapter includes an introductory paragraph that ends with the thesis or proposition, three body paragraphs that support the thesis, and a concluding paragraph that includes a restatement of the thesis.

The best way to support an argument is with adequate evidence, which is reliable, sufficient, and verifiable. Books, reference works (such as an almanac), and magazine articles can provide facts to use as evidence.

If you borrow facts or quotations from library resources, you must tell your readers where these references came from.

CHAPTER 10

A Tragedy Like This

Rocky Mountain News

DENVER, COLORADO
Tuesday, January 28, 1986

EXTRA

25¢

SHUTTLE EXPLODES

All 7 in Challenger crew die after liftoff

ASSOCIATED PRESS

The fireball that signaled disaster for shuttle mission 51-L occurred only 1 minute, 15 seconds after liftoff from Kennedy Space Center. NASA officials said there were no apparent problems at the time.

Newspaper and magazine articles and important paragraphs from books and reference works are used by student writers as parts of compositions, as references for research papers, and by themselves in **summarized** and **paraphrased** form. This chapter will help you tell the difference between summaries and paraphrases and will develop your skill in writing them.

WHAT IS A SUMMARY?

A *summary* is a condensation, or shortening, of the main ideas of another person.

It is written to give readers a clear idea of an article or book they may not have read. When writers summarize, they usually shorten several sentences into a summary of one sentence; a long paragraph can be summarized in two or three sentences, and several paragraphs can be summarized in a paragraph of four or five sentences. Summaries of longer selections may be several hundred words in length.

WHAT IS A PARAPHRASE?

A *paraphrase* states a single idea and its supporting details in about the same length as the original.

The following original article about the explosion of the U. S. space shuttle in 1986 and the summaries and paraphrase after it illustrate how to summarize and paraphrase.

Original article

The space shuttle tragedy struck the nation with shock and grief. Even those who saw the explosion and disintegration as they watched from the ground or in front of their television sets have difficulty believing that it actually happened.

America's space voyages have become so routine that people sometimes forget the risk inherent in such undertakings. It seems a long time ago when "Gus" Grissom, the corned-beef-sandwich eating astronaut, and two colleagues were burned to death in a fire on the launch pad in 1967. It is, in fact, 19 years and one day. Long enough to put aside the shock of that tragedy and to become almost nonchalant about our successive trips into space. . . .

"Tragic Loss of Space Shuttle Should Not Halt Exploration," *The Rocky Mountain News,*
29 January 1986, p. 44.

217

A Possible Three- to Four-Sentence Summary

The United States was shocked and saddened when the space shuttle exploded. No one could believe that it had actually occurred. Because so many space voyages have taken place successfully, people forget the dangers. In fact, the only other disaster happened in 1967.

A Possible Single-Sentence Summary

When the space shuttle exploded, the shocked people of the United States could not believe it because they had seen many successful voyages in the past.

A Possible Paraphrase

The United States was shocked and saddened when the space shuttle exploded. No one could believe that it had actually occurred. Because so many space voyages have taken place successfully, people forget the dangers. The only other space disaster happened in 1967 when three astronauts were burned to death as the result of a fire on the launch pad. The 19 years since that tragedy have made Americans confident about space travel.

QUESTIONS FOR CLASS DISCUSSION

1. What does the three- to four-sentence summary leave out of the original article? Are these details important to the understanding of the reader?

2. Does the three- to four-sentence summary begin in the same way as the original article? What word replaced *grief?* What single word replaced "those who saw the explosion and disintegration as they watched from the ground or in front of their television sets"?

3. What does the single-sentence summary leave out of the original?

4. How is the paraphrase different from the three- to four-sentence summary?

WRITING A SUMMARY

Follow the 12 steps below to help you write a good summary. Refer to these steps as you complete Exercise 10-1.

1. Read the article or section of a book once for general understanding.

2. Reread the article, this time looking for the author's main idea. If it is difficult to find the main focus of the article, turn the title into a question which you try to answer as you reread. Highlight or underline main ideas.

Make notes in the margin to summarize the main ideas of each paragraph in a few words. Use your dictionary to look up only those words that stop you from understanding the main idea.

3. Write a rough draft of your summary. One way to begin is to identify the author and title of the book or magazine.

EXAMPLE

> In an editorial entitled, "Tragic loss of space shuttle should not halt exploration," the writer states. . . .

> In *Politics USA,* John Scott discusses. . . .

4. Use your own words. Do not plagiarize. The only time you can use the author's exact words is when

> a. a word or words are the author's original term for a particular idea

EXAMPLE

The editor called it an "unsurvivable accident."

> b. you choose a particularly good statement from the original. When you use the author's exact words, you must connect these words with the author and place the words in quotation marks.

EXAMPLE

> "America's space voyages have become so routine that people sometimes forget the risk inherent in such undertakings," according to the author of the editorial.

> c. there is a word which has no synonym (*Europe,* for example) or very few synonyms (*space shuttle, research, international relations, solar energy*). If this is the case, you may copy the word.

5. Use your own writing style. Never use the author's exact word order or his style.

6. Use your own organization of ideas.

7. Do not add your opinions or ideas within the summary.

8. Include the major points made in the selection. If you are summarizing an entire article or chapter, include the conclusion reached by the author.

9. Leave out minor details, illustrations, anecdotes, and other unimportant material.

10. Use the same verb tense throughout your summary. Present tense is most often used for summaries of literature, past tense for biographies or history. In summarizing other forms of writing, choose a tense that seems to fit and use it throughout the summary.

11. A good summary is short, but still smooth and logical. Use linking words and expressons for smoothness.

12. State the author (if known), title of article or book, other publication information (date, publisher, place) either at the end of the summary or within the body of the summary.

EXERCISE 10-1   **Summarizing an Article**

Read the complete article on the space shuttle disaster. Paragraphs 1–6 have been summarized for you. Then follow the directions for summarizing paragraphs 7–14. Continue your summary on a separate sheet of paper.

Summary of Paragraphs 1–6

The United States was shocked and saddened when the space shuttle Challenger exploded in January 1986. No one could believe that it had actually occurred. Because so many space voyages have taken place successfully, people forget the dangers. In fact, the only other disaster happened in 1967. However, we must remember that the explosive strength needed to power the shuttle is always potentially dangerous, according to a *Rocky Mountain News* editorial entitled "Tragic loss of space shuttle should not halt exploration" (January 29, 1986).

1. Reread paragraphs 7 and 8. Summarize these short paragraphs into one sentence that says something about "the national loss."

2. Reread paragraph 9, which also states something about a national loss. Summarize this paragraph in one or two sentences. Add the summary to your summary of paragraphs 7 and 8.

3. Paragraph 10 talks about correcting whatever caused the explosion. It also gives the editor's opinion about stopping space exploration because of its danger. Write a summary that includes both of these ideas. Do not include details about Christa McAuliffe.

4. Reread paragraphs 11 and 12. These paragraphs talk about the benefits, or good points, of the space shuttle program. Summarize these benefits in three to five sentences.

5. Reread paragraphs 13 and 14. Paragraph 13 is the author's conclusion and states his opinion about astronauts. Paraphrase paragraph 13 and use it as the final paragraph of your summary. (Paragraph 14 lists names of astronauts killed in space shuttle disasters. These are details that can be left out of your summary.)

Tragic loss of space shuttle should not halt exploration

1   The space shuttle tragedy struck the nation with shock and grief.

    Even those who saw the explosion and disintegration as they watched from the ground or in front of their television sets have difficulty believing that it actually happened.

2   America's space voyages have become so routine that people sometimes forget the risk inherent in such undertakings. It seems a long time ago when "Gus" Grissom, the corned-beef-sandwich-eating astronaut, and two colleagues were burned to death in a fire on the launch pad in 1967. It is, in fact, 19 years and one day. Long enough to put aside the shock of that tragedy and to become almost nonchalant about our successive trips into space.

3   But danger is ever present when such enormous explosive forces are assembled to power mortal men and women and their tiny ship into the heavens.

4   Among those who watched through the many launch delays were schoolchildren from Boulder who won the trip, along with their teachers, in a Ball Aerospace competition for space-related proposals that could be used in classrooms. They, like other Americans, experienced momentary joy turned to disbelief and then grief.

5   Gone in the "unsurvivable accident" was University of Colorado graduate and mission specialist Ellison S. Onizuka. Lost, too, was the university's satellite Spartan Halley, which took two years and $5 million and was to study the composition of Halley's comet.

6   Colorado is also attached to the space program through Martin Marietta Aerospace, Inc., which has built all the external fuel tanks for the shuttle program at NASA's plant in Michoud, La.

7   But the tragic loss was national as well as personal.

8   Americans will not get to see the first truly civilian astronaut, teacher Christa McAuliffe, conducting classes from outer space. They won't get to see this enthusiastic woman emerge from a successful flight to tell the world of the wonders she saw.

9   A saddened President Reagan was right to postpone his State of the Union address and instead speak to the nation on the Challenger tragedy. A State of the Union speech, usually upbeat and filled with optimistic talk, would have been inappropriate on an evening when the nation was mourning lost astronauts.

10   Every attempt will be made to find out what caused the tragic malfunction of the spacecraft and to correct it. But Christa McAuliffe probably would be the first to say that the disaster that overtook Challenger's tenth flight should not cause the United States to halt exploration beyond the planet Earth. She knew the risks and was willing to compete with 11,000 others to be the first teacher in space. And she, like all the others, was a volunteer.

11   The space shuttle program has brought many benefits. Communications satellites have been launched. Biological experiments have been carried out. Tests have been made of construction methods for building a permanent space station in the future.

12   Perhaps most important, each voyage into space has given men and women additional knowledge of how to exist in an environment so alien to our own. As that knowledge accumulates, mankind will be able to expand its understanding of itself and of the universe and to advance the frontiers of science.

13   The men and women who have been the pioneers, and especially those who have lost their lives, in this undertaking are truly heroes and heroines.

14   Along with the names of Virgil Grissom, Edward White and Roger Chaffee, victims of that 1967 launch-pad fire, this nation now enshrines Christa McAuliffe, Judith Resnick, Francis Scobee, Michael Smith, Ronald McNair, Ellison Onizuka and Gregory Jarvis.

The Rocky Mountain News, Jan. 29, 1986, p. 44.

CHARACTER WORDS

Recognizing Character Words

Character words are an author's unique word choices. These words are part of the author's personality or style of writing; in a sense, they **belong** to the author. Therefore, these words must be changed when you summarize or paraphrase.

Here is an example from the previous article. The character words are in italics.

> "America's space voyages have become so *routine* that people sometimes forget the *risk inherent* in such *undertakings.*"

This sentence can be reworded in this way:

Because so many space voyages have taken place successfully, people forget the dangers.

How do you know which words are character words? They are almost always nouns, verbs, and specific adjectives and adverbs. Character words are ones the reader will probably remember because they are specific and eye-catching.

EXERCISE 10-2   Recognizing Character Words

In each of the following sentences, one or two words are unusual enough to be noticed and remembered. It is usually not a common word for a class of things, such as *machine* or *store* but a specific word such as *new-fangled device* or *supermall.* Circle these character words.

1. The automobile has become a suicidal conveyance.

2. Her eyes were riveted on the face of her teacher.

3. The sound of the jet engines was deafening.

4. When the president died, people in the street wept uncontrollably.

5. His monthly expenses were extravagant.

6. The countenance of the baby was beautiful and innocent.

7. What I do today is important because I am bartering a day of my life for it.

8. Hunger is the scourge of dry countries.

9. The stew of America is spiced by many cultures.

10. Aerospace engineers have begun to develop a rocket that will carry the United States into a new phase of space exploration and exploitation.

Changing Character Words

A character word can be changed either by replacing it with a synonym or expressing its meaning through a different structure.

Here are some examples:

Original: "Computers are essentially stupid."

The words *essentially* and *stupid* are unique to the author; they are character words. This sentence could easily be paraphrased by replacing these words with synonyms. *Essentially* could be exchanged for *basically* and *stupid* could be replaced by *dumb*.

Paraphrase: Computers are basically dumb.

Original: "Fiji. The name itself speaks of romance and tranquillity."

This sentence is structured in an unusual way, with the name of the country separated from the next sentence for emphasis. Also the words *romance* and *tranquillity* (and possibly even *speaks*) can be considered character words. This sentence is best rewritten with a different structure and replacements for the character words.

Paraphrase: Romantic love and serenity come to mind when one hears the
name "Fiji."

EXERCISE 10-3   Changing Character Words

Reread each of the 10 sentences in Exercise 10-2. Decide if the circled character words should be changed by replacing them, by changing the structure of the sentence, or both. Then rewrite each sentence on a separate sheet of paper.

ATTRIBUTING STATEMENTS TO THEIR SOURCE

When summarizing another's work it is important to let your readers know, early in the summary, from what source you have taken the information. This is called **attribution.**

For example, in the beginning of the summary, Exercise 10-1, the first paragraph ended with this statement:

However, we must remember that the explosive strength needed to power the shuttle is always potentially dangerous," according to a *Rocky Mountain News* editorial entitled "Tragic loss of space shuttle should not halt exploration" (January 29, 1986).

The underlined end of the previous sentence **attributes** the information to a specific editorial. The words *according to* at the end of the summary, the complete information about the editorial should be given.

> *A verb introduces the author or title of the statement.* Verbs you can use include:

states	writes
explains	comments
expresses	asks (used with question)
says	demands (used with strong request)
infers	according to

> *Commas come before the verb or phrase if the attributing phrase is at the end of the statement.*

> EXAMPLE

>> "Several major steps are involved in summarizing a paragraph", *explains Connie Shoemaker.* (These are the actual words of the author.)

> *No comma is necessary* if the verb or phrase used to attribute is followed by *that*.

> EXAMPLE

>> Connie Shoemaker explains *that* several major steps are involved in summarizing a paragraph.

EXERCISE 10-4   Using Attribution

Complete the following statements by adding words of attribution and any necessary punctuation.

EXAMPLE

"Love is blind" _____ proverb "A penny saved is a penny earned," expresses the value of thriftiness.

1. We've never had a tragedy like this _____ U. S. President

   Ronald Reagan. (These are the actual words of the president.)

2. _____ the United States has never experienced a tragedy

   like the explosion of the space shuttle.

3. People learn values _____ Clarence L. Ver Steeg in *World Cultures.*

4. Mu'ammar Al-Qadhafi is perhaps one of the most controversial contemporary political actors to have occupied the international stage during the past decade _____ Sami G. Hajjar, writing in *Africa Today.* (These are the actual words of the author.)

5. Trust is the degree of confidence you feel when you think about a relationship with another person _____ *Psychology Today.*

6. *Update magazine* _____ that most teenage marriages in the United States fail.

7. In their conversations, Americans often try to be relatively frank _____ *Culturegrams* (These are the actual words of the publication.)

8. A dream itself is but a shadow _____ Hamlet in the play by William Shakespeare. (These are the actual words of Hamlet.)

9. Hamlet _____ the unreal quality of dreams in the Shakespearean play.

10. American schools should be teaching more critical thinking _____ *Time magazine.*

EXERCISE 10-5   **Writing Summaries of Varied Topics.**

Review "Writing a Summary" on page 218. Using the steps listed there, write summaries for each of the following passages. Look for character words and replace them with synonyms or change the structure of the sentence.

1. Electricity is a property of nature that we usually know as electric current. We cannot see it, but we can see its effects. Rubbing two things together sometimes produces electricity. This happens when you take off a nylon sweater. The nylon rubs against your hair or your clothing. The electricity causes crackling and sparks. This effect has been known for thousands of years. A Greek philosopher called Thales noticed it in 600 B.C. He rubbed a piece of amber. When he did this, the amber tried to pull things towards it. This is because it had an electric charge. This is how electricity got its name. It comes from the Greek for amber, elektron.

> *The Raintree Illustrated Encyclopedia* (Milwaukee, Wisconsin: Raintree Publishers Ltd., 1979), p. 517.

2. Like time, space is organized differently according to different cultural patterns. Because Americans are taught to perceive and react to the arrangement of objects, we think of space as "empty." This is in contrast to the Japanese, who are trained to give meaning to spaces. The Japanese perception of shape and arrangement of what is to us empty spaces, appears in many aspects of their life. There appears to be a similarity between the culturally patterned perception of time and that of space. Just as North Americans think of time as being "wasted" unless one is doing something, so we think of space as wasted if it is not filled up with objects.

> Joan Gregg Young, *Communication and Culture* (New York: D. Van Nostrand, 1980), p. 60.

3. Centerpiece of the Muslim World, the Sacred Mosque at Mecca burgeons with life at the height of the pilgrimage season. Situated in an arid valley near the birthplace of Muhammed, the revered mosque, al-Masuid al-Haram, features seven minarets. At its center stands a 50-foot-high, cubelike stone structure called the Kaaba, which, according to Islamic tradition, is the shrine erected to God by Abraham. Some 800 million Muslims—about a fifth of mankind—turn toward this structure five times a day in prayer.

> Mohamed Amin, "Pilgrimage to Mecca," *National Geographic,* November 1978, p. 581.

4. How often have you said, "The day isn't long enough. . ." and then shuffled through your computer disks or stared quizically at your hard disk directories, trying to decide what work you should bring home. In fact, there is another—easier—way to bring your office work home: Link personal computers through a communications system. That way you can call up whatever files you need, as you need them, gain entry to the corporate mainframe or run remote applications, all without worrying ahead of time what to carry with you. And setting up the home-to-office connection is probably simpler than you imagine.

> Henry Fersko-Weiss, "Making the Home/Office Connection," *Personal Computing,* February 1986, p. 51.

5. Hospital x-ray technicians and nuclear-plant employees have long worn badges that monitor their exposure to radiation. But agricultural workers who handle deadly pesticides have had no way of knowing if they are being poisoned until they show symptoms. Now a green plastic badge developed by Robert E. Baier, a professor of biophysics at the State University of New York at Buffalo, may give farmers early warning. The badge contains a chemical that turns red upon contact. . . .

"A Badge That Monitors Pesticide Exposure," *Business Week,* February 24, 1986, p. 111.

6. The world's nuclear arsenal today stands at over 12,000 megatons (MT), enough to destroy 1 million Hiroshimas. Recent studies estimate that anywhere from 300 million to 1 billion people would be killed outright in a large-scale nuclear war and an equal number would suffer serious injuries requiring immediate medical attention—which would be largely unavailable. But what of the longer-term effects of nuclear war? What kind of world would survivors face? New evidence suggests that the long-term atmospheric and biological effects may be even more serious than the immediate ones.

United Nations Chronicle, January 1985, p. 45.

7. Remember your first few days—or weeks—away? Remember feeling like a fish out of water, no matter how broadminded you tried to be? Security props had been knocked out from under you. You wanted desperately to return home. Maybe you didn't even realize you were being affected, but you were. And so were those around you—maybe even seriously.

Remember how you thought and felt? Well, get ready for what may occur when you return home! You may suffer temporarily from what has been called "return shock." This may come as no surprise since "shocks" are common whenever we encounter a dramatic change, whether it is employment, housing, marital status, or moving. Even growing from childhood to adolescence produces "shocks." All forms of shock require a normal adjustment period.

"Coming Home Again: Absorbing Return Shock," *Infograms,* Brigham Young University, 1984, p. 1.

8. Lima, the capital of Peru, is a city with modern and old buildings and it has the largest Chinatown in the world, except for San Francisco's. It is also the city from which visitors take the plane to fly to the city of Cusco and then the road to Machu Pichu, the famous Indian ruins on the mountain top.

Alice Bonzi Mothershead, *Dining Customs Around the World* (Maryland: Garrett Park Press, 1982), p. 109.

9. Many movie actors and actresses are more famous than kings and presidents because millions of people all over the world watch movies. Hollywood, California, the capital of the movie industry, created the star system. A star is an actor or actress who is considered to be an outstanding performer, and who has

leading roles in movies. Charlie Chaplin was a famous pantomimist in silent films. Shirley Temple was one of the best-loved child actresses. Paul Newman and Elizabeth Taylor have both reached the top of their profession.

Students' Encyclopedia (Middletown, Connecticut: Xerox Corporation, 1980), p. 26.

10. You will probably find the most difficult part of the college selection process is trying to predict what will happen as a result of your decision. Will you be accepted by a college if you apply? Will you be happy at the "college of your choice"? Unfortunately, even good decisions cannot guarantee successful results. By its nature, decision-making involves risks. You will be in a better position, however, to judge the degree of risk and uncertainty if you do a thorough job of collecting and evaluating information.

The College Handbook: 1985–86 (New York: College Entrance Examination Board, 1985), p. xvii.

WRITING A PARAPHRASE

The previous exercise has given you practice in writing summaries of many different types of material: scientific, cultural, and so on. You may recall that summaries condense, or shorten, the main ideas of another person. Paraphrases are a bit different in that they state a single idea and its supporting detail in **about the same length** as the original.

The purpose of a summary and a paraphrase are different, too. A summary gives the reader enough information about the original article or book to let them decide if they want to read the original or it refreshes the reader's memory about the original. A paraphrase, on the other hand, helps either the writer or the reader to understand difficult material. For example, a paraphrase of technical material would use simpler terms to explain more technical ones. Or, a paraphrase of poetry would explain the poem in simpler language.

Many of the same techniques used in summarizing are used in paraphrasing. Use the following steps in writing a paraphrase:

1. Read the article or section of a book once for general understanding.

2. Reread the article, going over the material two or three more times, if necessary, until you understand it thoroughly. Find simple definitions for words you do not understand.

3. Put the original aside and write a rough draft of your paraphrase. Restate the ideas of the article or book in your own words. Do not use any of the original wording.

4. Check the original to be certain you have not left out any important ideas or have not misstated anything. Paraphrases are usually the same length as

originals although sometimes a paraphrase may need to be longer to fully explain any difficult ideas in the original.

5. Do not add your opinions or ideas within the paraphrase.

6. Follow the author's own organization of ideas. This should make your paraphrase easier to understand and more logical.

7. Include examples, illustrations, and anecdotes but be certain to reword them. Since the purpose of a paraphrase is to help someone understand the material, examples and details are important.

8. Use the same verb tense throughout your paraphrase.

9. State the author (if known), title of article or book, and other publication information (date, publisher, place) either at the end of the paraphrase or within the body of the paraphrase.

EXERCISE 10-6   Paraphrasing Passages

Write a paraphrase of each passage.

EXAMPLE

Religion was very important in the formation of the United States. The religious foundations upon which the country was built are still evident in some important ways today.

Paraphrase: When the United States began, religion was an extremely important force. These original religious beliefs are still obvious in the country today.

1. Yesterday's mission was the 25th in the shuttle program. It drew special interest because one of the seven aboard was the first "ordinary citizen" ever to head for space.

"Editorial," The Rocky Mountain News, Jan. 29, 1986, p. 3.

2. Music can move us to tears or to dance, to fight or to make love. It can inspire our most exalted religious feelings and ease our anxious and lonely moments.

Anne H. Rosenfeld, "Music, the Beautiful Disturber," Psychology Today,
December 1985, p. 48.

3. Success is counted sweetest
By those who ne'er succeed.
To comprehend a nectar
Requires sorest need.

Emily Dickinson, The Poems of Emily Dickinson (New York: Little, Brown
& Co., 1950), p. 120.

4. The most common type of lawsuit tried in American courts today is the damage suit arising out of the operation of automobiles.

> James Eichner, *Courts of Law* (New York: Franklin Watts, 1979), p. 1.

5. The biggest and most important of the thousands of soccer competitions is the Jules Rimet Trophy, commonly called The World Cup. This competition takes place in a different country every four years.

> Clive Toye, *Soccer* (New York: Franklin Watts, 1968), p. 4.

6. There is probably nothing—except perhaps your genes and your family—that shapes your life quite like government.

> Robert Lineberry, *Government in America* (Boston: Little, Brown & Co., 1980), p. v.

7. Gandhi's story is one of courage and determination and religious will.

> Gerald Gold, *Gandhi* (New York: New Market Press, 1983), p. 11.

8. Today the total of people in the world who speak English is 750 million. In other words, 1 out of every 7 people claims some knowledge of English.

> Susanna McBee, "English: Out to Conquer the World," *U. S. News & World Report,* Feb. 18, 1985, p. 50.

9. Cultural background is the single most powerful influence on our tastes for various foods because it steers us to certain combinations of foods and flavors.

> Paul Roxin, "Cultural Background Linked to Our Tastes," *Science Digest,* July 1984, p. 23.

10. Second only to General Grant as the greatest Northern commander in the Civil War was William Tecumseh Sherman.

> *Compton's Encyclopedia* (Chicago: F. E. Compton Co., 1980, p. 163.

EXERCISE 10-7 Summarizing from a Textbook

Choose two short paragraphs from one of your textbooks or from a textbook in your major field of study. Photocopy the paragraphs. Write a summary that is attributed to the book you have selected.

EXERCISE 10-8 Summarizing from a Magazine

Choose a short passage (a paragraph or series of paragraphs) from a magazine article of interest to you. Photocopy the passage. Write a summary of the passage. Include details of author, title of article, magazine, and date.

USING PARAPHRASING AND SUMMARIZING TO HELP YOU WRITE AN ESSAY

The ability to summarize and paraphrase is very helpful when you are faced with an assignment for which you need more than your own ideas. If you can find a selection from a book or magazine about your topic, you can summarize or paraphrase it and include it in your essay. Let's try your skills with the following assignment:

Writing Assignment

Write a two- to four-page essay that answers this question: *How has mass communication affected daily life in your country?*
    Follow the steps of the writing process.

Getting Ideas

You may wish to use listing or one of the brainstorming diagrams to record your ideas about the effects of radio, television, newspapers, and so on, on your country. After you have recorded ideas, visit the library to find a book or magazine that discusses mass communication's effects. This reference can do two things for you: give you more ideas and offer you information that can be summarized or paraphrased and used in your introduction or in other parts of your essay.

Listing, Brainstorming, and Freewriting

First, list all the ways in which radio, television, newspapers, magazines, and even billboards, have affected the lives of people in your country. Use a web like that used in previous exercises, showing the main idea in the center and other ideas branching out from it.
    You may also use listing or freewriting, in combination with brainstorming or alone, to get as many ideas as you need to begin your assignment.

Using Reference Tools

Next, read the following selection from the book *World Cultures,* by Clarence L. Ver Steeg (Glenview, Ill.: Scott, Foresman, 1977), pp. 332–333. After reading the selection, answer the questions that follow.

> Today, communicating is often more than simply trading ideas between a few people. Some media—such as television, radio, and newspapers—can bring messages to millions of people at one time. A football game on television might be watched by more than 50 million people. When a message is received by millions of people, we call this mass communication.
>   Mass communication can affect family life. In some countries television programs tell millions of people about family health care.

Mass communication can also affect people's values. They may use information communicated to them to form their ideas about what is good and what is not. For example, one leader in Turkey complained about today's communication media. He blamed them for luring people from the old agricultural way of life in Turkey to a new city way of living. To him, the city way of life was bad. Life in the crowded cities was too fast-paced. Cities had few established Turkish customs. Turkish farm people came to the city without a good idea of how to live there. The Turkish official said, "The course of the twentieth century is communications and newspapers. People cannot wait half a century to attain what they see in the pictures (of city life). We are becoming America—rush, rush, rush."

Mass communication also affects people's economic lives. In many countries, advertising is an important part of mass communication. Sellers use television, radio, newspapers, magazines, and billboards to get people to buy things like toys, cereals, food, floor cleaner, hair coloring, and cars.

Political leaders use the media of mass communication quite often. They use television and radio to tell their people about the government's ideas and plans. In fact, in some countries the government controls the media of mass communication. Very often in such countries, government leaders choose the information they think is proper for people to know. They allow only this information to reach most of the people.

1. What additional ideas did you get from the reading?

2. Have you already thought about the effect on family life? On people's values? On people's economic lives?

3. What about your government's use of television and radio?

4. Has this affected the lives of your people? In what ways?

Focusing on a Main Idea

Continue the writing process by studying your pattern of ideas and focusing on a thesis statement for your essay. The thesis should answer the question "How has mass communication affected daily life in my country?"

Writing the Rough Draft

Now it's time to write the rough draft of your essay. This is the point in the writing process when you can make use of the selection from *World Cultures*. Use the following steps to write your rough draft:

1. Paraphrase the definition of **mass communication** contained at the end of the first paragraph. This definition might make a good introductory statement for your essay: *When a message is received by millions of people, we call this mass communication.*

2. To further explain the term mass communication, you might want to add the examples given in the first paragraph of the reading—radio, television, and newspapers—to your paraphrase.

3. Now you can narrow down your introduction to the mention of your topic—"the effects of mass communication." If you recall, the main ideas of the second, third, fourth, and fifth paragraphs were "the effects of mass communication on areas of daily life." Write one or two sentences that summarize these effects.

4. Next put the pieces of the puzzle together: your definition and examples, the summary of effects and, finally, your thesis statement. You should have the first paragraph of your essay.

Here's how one student wrote the introductory paragraph:

Mass communication is the receiving of a message by millions of people through media such as radio, television, and newspapers. Mass communication can affect family life, people's values, and their economic lives. Political leaders also can use the media to influence its people in the way that the government chooses. Mass communication in my country, China, has had a strong effect on all four areas of our lives.

Continue to draft your essay. The plan of your composition should be clear in your first paragraph. For example, the student from China would first write about the effects of mass communication on family life, then people's values, and so forth.

Revising and Drafting Again

Revise and draft again. When completed, you should have an essay that uses ideas from an outside reference and examples from your own experience.

EXERCISE 10-9 Outlining the Composition

Outline the composition you have just written. The first division of the outline has been done for you in the outline form that follows.

The Effects of Mass Communication on _____

I. Introduction
   A. Definition of Mass Communication
   B. Possible Effects

      1. Family life
      2. People's values
      3. Economy
      4. Government control
   C. Effects of mass communication in my country

II. _____

_____

_____

_____

III. _____

_____

_____

_____

IV. _____

_____

_____

_____

V. _____

_____

_____

_____

VI. Conclusion

_____

_____

As you can see, the outline provides a kind of summary of your composition. If the parts of the outline seem to be in order and logically clear, you have a well-organized essay.

REVISION EXERCISES

REVISION EXERCISE 1 Adding Coherence to a Summary

Summarizing is like all good writing; it should result in smooth, logical paragraphs. The use of linking words and expressions, transitions between major ideas, results in coherence. Revise this summary about air pollution by adding linking words and phrases where needed or by combining short sentences into longer ones.

What Pollution Can Do

Air is considered to be polluted when it contains unnatural substances. Polluted air can destroy the balance of the exchange that goes on among plants, animals, and the oceans. Animals, including people, get necessary oxygen from the air they breathe. They exhale carbon dioxide. Plants need carbon dioxide to supply carbon for production of food. Plants draw in carbon dioxide, then release oxygen. Pollutants such as soot, sulfur, lead, automobile exhaust, and factory fumes poison the air. Over a long period of time, these pollutants could poison all forms of life.

Air pollution causes serious problems. Foul air damages crops. It wears away metals. Fumes in the air even eat away buildings made of stone. Pollutants cause holes in glass and kill grass and trees. People are affected most seriously. Pollution damages their health and shortens their lives.

REVISION EXERCISE 2 Using Summary and Paraphrase to Improve an Essay

You will be given the first two paragraphs of a student's essay on the educational system in his country. In addition to this, you will have a page from a reference book on the same topic. By paraphrasing and summarizing some material from the book, you can make additions to the student's essay that will improve it.

Read the student's essay and the selection from a book about Oman. Then follow the suggestions for revision. Write your revised version of the composition on a separate sheet of paper.

Nasir AL Riyami
Intermediate English
Professor Maxwell
December 12, 1988

Educational Changes in Oman

¹*Education has changed a lot in my country, Oman, in the last 15 years.* ²*In fact, it has changed more in these years than in all of the history before.* ³*In this paper, I would like to discuss how the changes in government of my country have changed the whole system of education.*

⁴*The Sultanate of Oman occupies most of the southeastern part of the Arabian peninsula.* ⁵*It is bordered on the northwest by the United Arab Emirates, on the west by Saudi Arabia, on the southwest by the Peoples' Democratic Republic of Yemen.* ⁶*In its early history, Oman had only religious schools and a few private schools.* ⁷*There weren't many students enrolled before 1970 and girls couldn't go to school.* ⁸*When oil was discovered in 1962, some families could afford to send their children to school outside the country, but nothing really happened to the educational system until eight years later.*

EDUCATIONAL SYSTEM

History

The date of July 23, 1970 marks a turning point in the history of education in Oman. On that date a coup stripped Sultan Said bin Taimur of power and placed his son Sultan Qaboos bin Said at the head of the government, bringing a radical change in the government's attitude toward education.

Prior to that time the *kutab,* or religious schools which taught verses of the Koran by rote, predominated. Aside from these classes and several private schools, education in Oman before 1970 was restricted to the primary level at three schools located in Muscat, Mutrah, and Salalah. The total enrollment was 909 boys. There was no education beyond this level and none at all for girls. In fact, there was no educational strategy for developing Oman, even after the discovery of oil in 1962. Students whose families could afford it went into self-imposed exile abroad to obtain the education denied them in Oman.

Under Sultan Qaboos the growth of education has been explosive. . . . In the first year of the Sultan's rule, the number of primary schools increased from three to sixteen, including three for girls. Popular demand for education has outstripped the development of facilities. In the early days, to accommodate classes until permanent facilities could be built, tents, huts, and mobile units sprang up wherever a teacher was available. Children in the interior and rural areas often walked long distances to schools or stayed with relatives in an urban area. Enthusiasm for education has spread throughout the country and touched all levels of society. While not compulsory, education is free and actively encouraged.

During the first phase of development from 1970 to 1975, education was extended to towns and villages. The number of schools rose dramatically from three primary schools in 1969–70 to 163 primary schools, 11 preparatory schools, and 2 secondary schools in 1974–75. During the same period, school enrollments increased manifold from 909 students to 49,229. The female student population, which did not have access to formal education in Oman prior to 1970, had grown significantly in numbers, totaling 12,378 at the close of this phase.

The second phase, from 1976 to 1980, marked a period of planned growth during the first Five-year Plan. The educational structure was defined; the curriculum was designed with the assistance of UNESCO and Jordanian and Egyptian consultants; the preparation of educational materials appropriate for Omani students (often called the "Omanization of the curriculum") was started, initially with an emphasis on developing materials for primary school students; and school facilities (buildings, laboratories, and teacher housing) were rapidly built or improved to meet the growing educational needs of the country. At the close of this phase, there were 237 primary schools, 114 preparatory schools, and 12 secondary schools. Enrollment statistics for 1980 show a total school population of 94,823 students, of whom 29,868 were females.

Other notable developments included the establishment of specialized education in critical areas: the Teacher Training Institute (for primary school teachers); the Agricultural Institute; vocational training centers, and two model preparatory schools with a technical emphasis.

The Admission and Academic Placement of Students from Bahrain, Oman, Qatar, United Arab Emirates, Yemen Arab Republic (Washington, D. C.: The Joint Committee on Workshops, National Association for Foreign Student Affairs, 1984), p. 43.

1. Sentence 3 of the student's essay expresses his thesis or main idea. The student says what he would like to do rather than doing it. Revise the wording of this sentence to focus on changes in government making changes in education.

2. Sentences 1 and 2 show that the student has focused on the idea that education in Oman has made rapid changes in 15 years. Using some of the facts from the reference book on Oman might make this introduction more interesting than the general things said by the student. Paraphrase the first

paragraph of the reference to use as an introduction, replacing sentences 1 and 2 of the student's essay.

3. Now you're on your own! Consider how you can revise the second paragraph. Use facts from the reference to help you in this revision. (Paragraph two in the reference is particularly helpful for facts about the early days of education in Oman.

4. Write a third paragraph that is a summary of the third paragraph of the reference. Is there a statement there that might make a good direct quotation? If so, place it in quotes and attribute it to its source. (Since the title of this book is very long, you might just refer to it as "a publication of the National Association for Foreign Student Affairs.")

5. Write a final paragraph using statistics, in summary, from the third and fourth paragraphs of the reference. The purpose of this paragraph is to show factually how numbers of schools and numbers of students have grown from 1970 to 1980. Do not try to include all of the statistics, just a selected few to prove your point.

6. Add a sentence or two of conclusion, possibly restating the thesis about the growth of education and changes in government.

FOR WRITERS WHO HAVE MORE TO SAY

Class Assignment

Write a composition, similar to the revision exercise, that discusses the growth of education in your country. Use one library reference as a resource for the paper.

CHAPTER SUMMARY

Two skills frequently used by student writers are summarizing and paraphrasing.

Summarizing condenses, or shortens, the main ideas of another writer.

Paraphrasing states a single idea in about the same length as the original writing.

When a writer summarizes or paraphrases, it is important to attribute the material to the source from which it was taken.

Summarizing and paraphrasing help the writer to avoid *plagiarism,* which means stealing and using the writings of another person as one's own writing.

EDITING CHECKLIST

Instructions: Each time a composition is marked by the instructor and returned to you, enter the date of the composition and one word that indicates the topic. Review the suggestions made by the instructor and check (√) the area of the chart that applies to your mistake. When you edit your next composition, refer to this checklist.

Date/Topic												
CONTENT												
Knowledge of Topic												
Development of Main Idea												
Interest												
Other Comments												
ORGANIZATION												
Outline												
Introduction												
Main Idea/Thesis												
Supporting Details												
Conclusion												
Method of Development												
Unity												
Other												
VOCABULARY												
Word Choice												
Word Form												
Other												
LANGUAGE USE												
Agreement Subject-Verb												
Agreement Pronoun												
Articles												
Pronoun Ref./ Antecedent												
Verb Choice (Tense)												
Prepositions												
Word Order												

EDITING CHECKLIST (cont.)

Date/Topic										
LANGUAGE USE (cont.)										
Transitions										
Shift of Person, number, tense Parallelism										
Sentence Variety										
Other										
MECHANICS										
Spelling										
Punctuation										
Capitalization										
Paragraphing										
Handwriting										
Other										

MY LIST OF FREQUENTLY MISSPELLED WORDS

1. _____
2. _____
3. _____
4. _____
5. _____
6. _____
7. _____
8. _____
9. _____
10. _____

11. _____
12. _____
13. _____
14. _____
15. _____
16. _____
17. _____
18. _____
19. _____
20. _____

Acknowledgments

p. 1, The Mansell Collection Ltd.   *p. 2,* The Bettmann Archive   *p. 25 (top),* Minoru Aoki/Photo Researchers; *(bottom),* Stuart Cohen   *p. 26 (top),* Connie Shoemaker; *(bottom),* Linares/Monkmeyer Press   *p. 45,* Ken Heyman/Archive Pictures, Inc.   *p. 48,* Roberta Hershenson/Photo Researchers, Inc.   *p. 69, (top and bottom),* and *p. 70,* Kit Miniclier   *p. 93,* Ken Heyman, Archive Pictures, Inc.   *p. 94,* Kit Miniclier   *pp. 108, 206, 207, The World Almanac & Book of Facts,* 1986 edition, © Newspaper Enterprise Association, Inc., 1985, New York, NY 10166   *p. 116,* Kit Miniclier   *p. 126,* Connie Shoemaker   *p. 138 (top)* Laimute E. Druckis/Taurus Photos; *(bottom),* Hugh Rogers,/Monkmeyer Press   *p. 167,* AP/Wide World Photos   *pp. 164, 165, 179, From The World Book Encyclopedia,* © 1986 World Book, Inc.   *pp. 193, 194,* U.S. Navy photographs   *pp. 205–209,* Reprinted by permission of the Putnam Publishing Group from *Mixed Company: Women in the Army* by Helen Rogan. Copyright © 1981 by Helen Rogan   *p. 215,* AP/Wide World Photos   *p. 221,* Reprinted by permission of *The Rocky Mountain News*   *pp. 236–237,* From *The Admissions and Academic Placement of Students from: Bahrain, Oman, Oatar, United Arab Emirates, and Arab Yemen,* p. 43; reprinted by permission of the American Association of Collegiate Registrars and Admissions Officers and the National Association for Foreign Student Affairs